UNFOLLOW
THE
CROWD

UNFOLLOW THE CROWD

The New Education for Young Millennials Who Crave Purpose, Freedom & Impact.

By Jarrod Uddin

Copyright © 2017 by Jarrod Uddin

ISBN - 978-1539973942

ISBN - 1539973948

Manufactured in the United States of America.

CONTENTS

DEDICATION

To The Village.

I dedicate this book to "the village": My family, friends, teachers, and mentors. Everyone who ever believed in me, had a hand in raising me, sharpening me, coaching me or toughening me up. To everyone who has made an invaluable deposit of wisdom into my life so that I could be the person I am today. Your investment came without conditions or a price tag. Thank you all for your invaluable contribution so that I could be the best me possible for the purpose of serving others. It means everything to me! Thank you all!

To My Fellow Millennials.

We are the generation that would stay in our parents' basements or even opt to be homeless before we took a job doing something that we are not passionate about, or work for someone or someplace where there was no purpose, impact or future. We are a generation determined to rewrite our destinies and outrun the who and what we are expected to be. And within these pages lies the formula.

INTRODUCTION

Why Not ME?

There was nothing super special about me. I had no lucky breaks in life and I hadn't won any genetic lottery. But by the time I was 23, I had already lived the kind of life that most people would only dream about. I had performed audience warmups for syndicated television. Dined with celebrities and global leaders. Built three successful small businesses from scratch. Performed in commercials and in a major motion film. I had spoken to nearly 100,000 students in combined audiences nationwide. I became a TEDx speaker and had trained multiple school districts of educators on how to be better teachers. I felt like a rock star. I was traveling the country, living my dream and making a difference. But the mountaintop is not where my journey began.

I had just graduated from college and had the option to enter into corporate America. Work a desk job with the potential to earn a fairly decent living. But the thought of punching the clock every day, putting in 8-hours of work that would bore me to tears, was depressing. So instead, I declined. And I paid the price by spending the first 9-months after my college graduation, homeless. Sleeping in my car. Occasionally couch surfing and doing everything I could to survive and figure out my life. It was sometimes miserable, but well worth the struggle looking back.

In retrospect, I have always done the things that others were afraid to do. Stayed in the game when others opted for the exit. Against my better judgement, I have assumed levels of courage and strength that I didn't think I had, in order to achieve the things that I really wanted. And the audacity to pursue the dreams and goals that kept me awake at night. Beyond my limitations. Beyond my fears and hesitations. My entire life has been about taking big risks for the chance at being better and having better. Each time against society's norms and conventionalisms. Against what my family and friends thought about my choices. All for the chance to pursue the dreams and goals inside of me that I inherently knew that I had to do something about.

An Interview with Your Fear:

Fear will always be there. There are hundreds of seminars every year that aim to help people eliminate fear. But there is something about fear that is to be respected. Fear can be a teacher of sorts. And it will always be in your life. Not to be eliminated, but to be learned from. Fear is not your enemy. Your choice not to deal with it is the real enemy. Sit down next to it and seek understanding. Ask the tough questions. *What is it saying? What is this fear trying to teach me about myself?* Maybe it's pushing you to take action in spite of the unknown. Maybe it's reminding you of a relationship that is really important, along with the overdue apology that you need to deliver.

Stop Wishing

'Wishing' that you could do or have something has a way of robbing you of any and all possibility that you CAN. It convinces you to believe in the myth of your shortcomings and limitations rather than your abilities. It blinds you into self-imposed defeat before attempting your first shot. Even if the competition appeared to be smarter, sharper, older, faster or better, those realities have never stopped me from a bold pursuit. When it comes down to something that you really want. A dream or goal that resonates within your heart's desire. A goal so big that you count yourself out in advance, ask yourself: *Why not ME?*

In college, the position of Campus Ambassador was the highest male dominated seat on my University's Student Government Association. To earn the position, one would have to be nominated by their peers, run a full fledge campaign, compete in a 5-scene stage competition in front of an audience of 3,000 of their peers (and a panel of judges), and acquire the majority share of votes from the student body. People would sometimes invest years into planning out their campaigns and spend the multiple thousands of dollars often required to run such an operation. I never thought that could be me, nor did I believe I would ever have the courage to step foot on a stage in front of thousands of my peers. But seeing the impact that this kind of leadership position could have on policies and in the lives of students and after identifying the intersection of their needs and my talents, I finally challenged myself with the question: *Why not ME?*

The ambassadorship was a position that people convinced me was reserved for those that were smarter, taller, better looking and infinitely more popular than me. Nevertheless, against convention, popular belief or impending obstacles, I went for it, and won. That position allowed me to make a serious impact, not just on campus, but in the surrounding community, and has granted me access to global leaders, U.S Presidents (and nominees), some amazing friendships, insanely phenomenal experiences, and memories that will last me a lifetime.

The Proof

Oftentimes, we miss out on what could be the greatest opportunities of our lives to learn, grow, advance or make a serious impact, because we are waiting on too much *proof* before we take the next step. Proof that we have the support. Proof that we are smart enough. Creative enough. Liked by enough people. Why doesn't everyone just go after the things they really want in life? It usually involves a series of life's labels and harmful experiences have taught us that we are not good enough to pursue or possess the things we really want. That we don't deserve the desires that ring the truest in our hearts and minds because of our mistakes, shortcomings or where we come from.

And then there are the societal expectations. Previous rejections. The voices of parents and the people closest to us who might say: *You're too young. You don't have the experience. Well you know, just about the majority of people who attempt that, fail. Why don't you come up with a Plan B?* The voices of sometimes well-meaning people who will try and back you out of pursuing what could end up being your greatest accomplishments. In the name of playing it 'safe'.

Our generation has a tendency to spite previous generations for not properly preparing us for life, or for not being who we wanted them to be or what we needed them to be. The same is true when it comes to our bosses, managers or team leaders. We can often hold them to incredibly high or unfair standards and expect them to maintain those parameters. But rarely are we willing to level up to those same ideals, while being willing to listen, learn, remain teachable and focus past their imperfections, missteps and humanity.

How we treat those around us or assigned to seats of authority over us will dictate what comes back to you. Even when it comes down to someone we don't like, value or even someone we don't believe has earned our respect. The Golden Rule is in still in full effect. I have always lived by this mantra. What you put out in the atmosphere will come back to you in spades! Treat others well and others will treat you well. Whether you call it the trifecta, The Law of Reciprocity, The Golden Rule, etc, the principle is real. The reverse is also true. Give everyone a chance. Forgive them for their humanity and imperfections. What goes around comes around.

But we all have that "something" that resonates inside of us. Call it a gut instinct. Intuition. Purpose. An honest desire to do better. Have better or become better. A dream that we can visualize internally but just don't know what to do or how to get there. A desire to be engaged in the kind of work that expresses and compliments the very best of who we are or would like to become. The desire to live happily ever after. If we're being honest, these are the things that eat away at us and keep us up at night when we are not engaged in full-on dream pursuit.

I urge you to pay careful attention to those things that are tugging at you in your moments of quiet! There will be some desires that resonate so deeply within you that you will find yourself unable to commit to anything else until you do something about them. What are your deepest desires? What are the dreams or goals that have been keeping you up at night? What is it that you are willing to risk everything for? When you can answer that, then you know you've got something worth pursuing and fighting for. It will cause you to take the leap against all popular opinion and do something audacious, bold, and daring, because what's inside you is greater than the confines of peer pressure and convention. And that is always worth the risk required.

YOU ARE HERE FOR A REASON

Quite Frankly, I believe that every individual on the planet was born for a reason and programmed with a special set of traits, talents, personality, look, and is supposed to perform a certain work before they die. Period. I believe that each and every one of us has an extremely unique combination of abilities that will aid us in getting our greatest work into the world. I believe therefore, that one of the greatest dangers is in comparing yourself to other people who you may believe have something you don't. Using that as your excuse for inaction. Yes, others will have traits, skills and abilities that you may not. But so do you! Everyone is uniquely and adequately supplied to make their own special dent in the universe, and you are indeed perfectly equipped to make yours!

Deep down, we all have some sort of dream inside of us. A path that you are supposed to be on. Some sort of work you are supposed to be doing. You may not see the entire picture in all of its detail and implicit instruction, but you know that there is indeed something you're supposed to do in life. Something that sets you apart (even if only by a small fraction - I call this "the it factor"). Something that is going to make you happy and compliment whatever unique talents and strengths that you have. Something that you are going to be doing one day that the world will benefit from. You may not even be able to explain it, write it, or do it. But you know it's there. You know that the potential is in you. You know that there's a path. You know it's out there. And you know it because you can "feel it".

You can feel it in those rare moments of quiet time. When you go to bed at night. When you're losing sleep. When you're in a class or on a job that bores you to tears (or someplace that has nothing to do with the "direction" that you feel you should go in). And the crazy thing, is you don't even have a clear enough picture or plan of pursuit, (it's like chasing an invisible target that only you can see) but you know deep down it's worth the chase! It's worth the pursuit. It's worth the brunt of your family and friends calling you "crazy". It's worth whatever you have to sacrifice in order to explore and find it. You need only get in pursuit.

But on the other side of that dogmatic effort and sacrifice, criticism and pain of pursuit, is victory. Dream moments await you there. Everything you want is on the other side of what you won't do. Or on the other side of what others won't do. This is the heart of 'Unfollow The Crowd'. Identifying your dreams and being relentless in your pursuit. Which also means applying constant pressure on your efforts towards the things you want in life. It will not fall in your lap. It will require strict and focused effort.

But I PROMISE you, it will also be the most rewarding push you will ever make. You will enjoy the sacrifice. It is an easy burden because it will fueled by passion. The purpose inside of you will fuel and empower you. You'll find yourself spending hours on your craft and won't even realize it. And it is that craft in combination with your heart and dogmatic effort that will change the hearts and minds of the world. It's the thing that the world will admire, love and respect. Not the "version" of yourself that we're often peer-pressured into becoming. Or the manufactured "script" that others have written for our lives.

What dream life, career or plan would you pursue (with all of your effort) if you knew that there was NO way that you could fail? Better yet, what dream is deep inside of you, that you would pursue if you knew you would fail, but would nonetheless pursue because the thought of never having attempted it would drive you crazy? The thought of watching others live their dreams while yours pass you by. To see someone else one day living a dream that you knew you could've had, but backed out of.

You owe it to yourself to try. To go after it. Even if the probability of failure is high. Do it anyway! There is a difference between failure and quitting. Quitting often involves changing lanes, reevaluating your choices, true motives, resources required and then choosing differently. Failure on the other hand is completely giving up on your direction in life. It's resigning from ever trying again. Of course, you'll get challenged, maybe even knocked down, or face setbacks that knock the wind out of you. This happens to the best of us. But when it does, take a breather and rest up. But by all means, do not stay there! Hurry up and get back up and stay in pursuit.

Again, there's nothing super special about those who do achieve their dreams. Might they have things that you don't? Of course. But the greatest difference is their decision to take the leap and pursue their desires in spite of opposition. In spite of challenges and failed attempts.

There is no Roadmap. But there is a Path

Growing up, I knew that I loved to read, write and speak. In school, English, Writing and Public Speaking were my favorite subjects, even from the First Grade. I didn't know why, but I knew that as long as I was doing these three things, I would be happy for the rest of my life. I later began to believe that my "calling" in life was to be a journalist, reporter and newscaster, because it was the one career I found that would allow me to express all three of those proclivities.

It wasn't until after three news internships that I realized the world of reporting the news was not for me. I later discovered that my REAL path was to speak, author and mentor people younger than me. Once I began to pursue that path, the real rewards began to come. I've had and continue to have DREAM moments that don't even compare to the path I thought I was originally supposed to pursue. All of this is available for you too. The more action you take in pursuit of what's inside of you, the more your path will unfold. The more the picture will reveal.

There is no roadmap for this. So within these pages, I am not going to promise you one. Just a set of choices that I have followed, and even those of other greats. But it will NEVER be revealed all at once! You have to stay in constant pursuit for the grand picture to unfold.

I want you to start thinking about your desires, your truest strengths, talents and abilities. The things that you find yourself engaged in for hours on end. The hobbies and activities that you retreat to. The things that come easy to you but difficult to others. The things that others say you are amazing at. Within those things, lie your clues and details to your purpose roadmap.

Skip The Party:

What will ultimately set you apart from the "crowd" is your willingness to ambitiously pursue those things, while others simply choose not to. When you are in pursuit of goals that are shaped around your purpose, you will begin to notice that there are opportunities all around you to exercise your talents and strengths. Places and occasions that will give us a platform to express the best of who we are.

This kind of pursuit may just require missing some parties. Some hanging out and frivolous time wasting. I'm not telling you to give up your life, but if we're being honest, most of us waste a lot of time doing nothing of value or true substance. Back in school, if I were to sacrifice going to just one party (which was essentially 5-6 hours of drinking and another 18 hours of next-day recovery), I could have achieved a ton more in that full 24-hour window (and actually felt great about waking up the next day).

'Unfollowing the crowd' means being willing to do what others will not, to live a life like most people never will. Period. It means potentially having to say NO to a ton of other convenient distractions and entertainment that are quite frankly a pointless time suck.

Don't miss your divine moments

The day I took the plunge, was the day that my life changed. I was on my way to the airport (after 9-months of being homeless) to go to D.C. My aunt had hooked me up with a desk job with the company she worked for and I agreed to give it a try. Although I was grateful, deep down I *knew* it wasn't ME. I knew I had other passions, talents and an idea of what I wanted for my life. I just didn't know WHERE I could get paid to DO what I loved, however, what I did know is that this pending job, was not it!

This may not be your story, but we all arrive at these points in life where we are challenged with answering the hard questions: *"Who am I? Where do I belong? What should I be doing with my life?"* We all suffer with these crossroads at various points of our lives, particularly during periods of intense life change: Being fired from a job. College graduation. After a failed relationship, etc. You only suffer with these hard questions when you are stagnant in your pursuit. Or when you have been wasting time not doing anything that matters to you, or anything that advances the lives of other people. When everything has always been "all about you" you will always feel empty, depleted and unfulfilled. Shallow goals like *making a lot of money* shouldn't be your highest pursuit. What you can do for others should be your goal. When passion and purpose meet, the money will follow.

Nevertheless, we will still come to places on our journey where we are faced with these questions that we will have to answer and choices that we must make in the moment, based on nothing more than a gut feeling. That day, all I knew is that in my gut, the D.C move was NOT the right choice.

It was right in that moment, right when I thought I was stuck with no way out, that an idea came to me! I remember a cousin of mine urging me to stop by a particular agency in the city that was on the way to the airport. Right then I remembered her saying that they are always looking for people with my skills set to travel, speak and do sales. It was a long shot. I didn't want to be late for my flight, but I knew this could potentially be my last chance. The opportunity that I always wanted. A shot to finally get paid to do what I really loved. The agency was only two exits away, and in a moment's notice, I decided to get off of the freeway and head in.

Long story short, I made the right choice. I ended up getting an on-the-spot interview, and hired immediately! I was living the dream, paid to travel the country and speak. I was finally doing the work that I felt I was *born to do*. The road hasn't always been easy but I've been living my dream ever since, and that's what I want for YOU! That visceral feeling that comes when you see an opportunity, and decide that your potential might actually be worth taking a chance on. There's no feeling like THAT moment. In all honesty, I had no idea what would happen for me. But I knew there was no way that I could ignore the shot if given the chance.

I absolutely believe that there are places that you just have to "show up" to in order for the "magic to happen". Quite honestly, most people are stuck in life because they think too long, are waiting on too much proof that 'it will work out' before they just get started. What I know for sure is that the entire picture is NEVER revealed to you upfront or before you begin your pursuit.

Getting the 'good stuff' is going to require a plunge. It will require jumping in with both hands and feet at a moment's notice. There are times where it will require total submission to the wisdom of a mentor, quick decisioning and acting fast if you are going to stand a chance at capitalizing on the moment. There are times when your situation will leave zero room for hesitation, deep thought or consideration. Opportunities that you must be prepared to seize in a moment's notice! Moments that often do not come back a second time around.

But what if I fail?

But what if 'no attempt' means missing out on the best thing that could ever happen to you?

I'll level with you here. Fear of failure isn't where it begins. Fear of failure is always the outgrowth of something deeper. We have all at times been unfairly labeled, beaten down to some extent by life's experiences and have learned not to try. Experiences that have taught us to approach things or even relationships with some hesitation, distance or mistrust. Or to quite simply, play it safe and not try at all.

Personally, I would rather you take that risk that maybe you were born to do something phenomenal than choose to do nothing, compromise, settle, and then arrive at the end of your life looking back on a life that you could have lived. I would rather you aim, shoot and miss (100-times) than to obey your fear. You have no idea what your limitations are until you take the plunge and give it your best shot.

Your Wings Do Work

What holds us back from these moments quite honestly? Are those life experiences that have taught us that our "wings won't work" if we take the leap. Your wings DO work and this book urges you to begin exploring the things that hold you back from making bold and courageous moves. From believing in yourself. The labels that have been unfairly assigned to you. The negative and harmful experiences that have been invited upon us. This is required internal work to be able to live authentically as that bold and daring phenom that the world is going to see you as.

What saddens me the most is seeing people unsatisfied with their lives. Pursuing majors that bore them. Clocking into jobs that they feel are soul-deadening. Having an understanding of what it is that they really want to do, but are so afraid of failing, that they never take the risk required in doing something about it. Or just feel that they are too far down the path of "adulthood" (mortgage, bills, student loans, job tenure), to either start over, turn the corner or explore a new route.

'Unfollowing the crowd' will at times require you to defy convention. It means launching before you're ready. It means taking a chance on yourself and trusting that you are smart enough to figure things out as you go. It means constantly staring down your fears, weaknesses, drugs of choice, acute insecurities and sharpening your resolve. It means consistently examining and learning about yourself and dealing with what's holding you back so that you can be the best demonstration to the world that you can become. You are your own best teacher about yourself. And you will be learning more about yourself and your purpose until the day you take your last breath. It will, for the rest of your life, continue to unfold until the day you die or decide to "retire from life".

'Unfollowing the crowd' is means writing your own story. It may even mean losing some friends along the way who aren't ready to walk that path with you. But the path you end up forging will be your own. It means listening to your gut and following your intuition. It's what will cause you to make the most impact in the world. Your unique dent in the universe. Create a legacy and have a story worth telling!

To offer you a step by step guide to purpose would rob you of the experience of becoming who you are. Instead, I offer you an intense invitation into the unknown where you will have to follow your inner compass. Your intuition. Your gut. I am not providing a roadmap, rather a set of truths, principles, and required choices along with my story. Everyone's destination is unique which makes your path oblique yet custom fit.

Do Not Retire

Quite simply put, I do not believe in retirement, because there is always more! Even when you think you've peaked in life, you're still learning and growing. As long as you are still living and breathing, there is always more to do. More to learn. More impact to make. More purpose left inside of you. Until I take my last breath, I will always be in pursuit of some new goal.

YOUR EGO IS NOT YOUR FRIEND

I've found that one of the biggest reasons that we pursue success is to prove to someone else that we could. To the people that may have doubted us. The people that discarded us or counted us out. The people whose harmful words or actions made us feel as if we could not do, have or become something better. Oftentimes, these life experiences either beat us down into fear and inaction, or they can become our fuel to be better and do better. To prove to others that we are indeed "good enough".

That would be your ego taking you for "a ride". Your ego is your inner voice of envy, competitive jealousy and insecurity that convinces you to do things, not for the betterment of other people, but for selfish and personal validation. It's the voice that convinces you to buy the new outfit. The new car that you cannot afford. Or convinces you to pursue success only for how you might be viewed, envied or perceived by others. I caution you, do not make your purpose about proving to "someone else" that you're good enough or worthy. Your true motivation for success should always be for the people whose lives that your purpose will ultimately serve and purely driven by the desire to get your greatest work into the world. Because in the end, it is your service to advance humanity that will make you great.

I am no exception to this standard. At one point, I was victim to my ego and in career pursuit for the money. The fame. What the spotlight would do for my ego. For the people who treated me as if I wasn't good enough. So that they would have to see me succeed and ultimately swallow back their harmful words and doubts.

I realized that my greater reason needed to be about the people who were looking up to me. That's who I am in pursuit for. For those who are struggling to find direction and uncovering their own paths in life. For those who are at the precipice of their own breaking points. For those whose lives are hanging in the balance of a moment where they will have to choose and decide on what path to take and who they will become. That is my motivation. Ego aside. I know my WHY. And that purpose carries a much greater motivation, fulfillment, happiness and reward than my ego could ever provide.

As for the people who doubted me, my sharpening has taught me to rather forgive those who discounted me, threw me away or didn't believe in me. That's the internal work… (more on this later) Within these pages lies stories, choices, instructions (even motivation) to help you achieve and become the best possible human being you can become. You will also be successful. But I warn you: Achieving success has a way of making us lazy. Because you will have already established yourself as being "good enough".

DON'T PURSUE SUCCESS. PURSUE PURPOSE.

Purpose is a much higher calling than success. Purpose will take you into places and have you doing work that you never dreamed of. Purpose is about other people benefiting from what you uniquely do (even if you have yet fully developed into that person). Success will reward you with money, accolades and things, while purpose will change lives, establish your legacy and memory, and create a unique footprint in this world with your name on it. A footprint that will hallmark and impact lives long after you're gone.

When we are in success pursuit and not purpose, we won't value our lives as we should. We become more easily exposed to anxiety, disappointment, depression, and even suicidal thoughts. Did I mention recklessness? Which in my opinion is a close cousin of 'suicide'. I can't tell you the number of people who are walking around aimlessly in life, feeling as if they have zero direction, depressed, living life on the edge just to be able to 'feel something', and if they just so happen to die, so be it.

But when you begin to do the internal work prescribed within these pages and identify your purpose (the intersection of your talents and the needs of others) your life immediately becomes more valuable to you. It becomes precious and worth whatever price is required to protect it! You'll even eat healthier, take more precaution and steer clear of life threatening activities and dangers. When we don't value our lives we become reckless with limited caution or care. And your purpose MUST be stronger than just proving someone else wrong, competing with your contemporaries. What if that PERSON one day dies? Then along with them die's your purpose for pursuit. And purpose is too important to hinge on something so small.

SOW SOME SEEDS. PLANT A FOREST. CREATE A LEGACY.

When I was growing up, there was a buzz phrase among my teachers. They called us the *microwave generation*. Meaning they believed us to be the generation that wanted everything instantly. Hungry? No need to go kill the fatted calf, skin it, butcher it or spend the 16-hours required to slow cook a meal. Just grab a hot pocket or some pizza rolls and have them ready in 5-minutes. Easy. Besides, who really wants to wait, struggle and fight for fulfillment or pleasure when it can be had almost instantaneously?

That's how many of us were wired. To believe that if we wanted something, that it should be instant, without having to work too hard, wait too long, train hard, receive rejection or wait in line.

But there are some things in life that require just that, and have zero guarantees. Things like: A happy marriage, a fulfilling career, smart kids, mile-deep friendships. These things require a different mindset, and the long haul is essential. The time investment is required. There's no app for great relationships. There's no Swipe right for the truly valuable things that really matter in life. There are some things that you will be able to fast track and make quantum leaps and bounds on, but most things that are worth having, will be arduously built, slow and difficult to attain. And there is no way around this. Most of your contemporaries really just want it easy. They don't truly want to put in the work. Their subconscious autopilot is steering them towards comfort. Towards the path of least resistance. True fulfilment never comes this way. There's no microwave for that.

I remember reading a story about the Swedish Navy receiving a letter from the Forestry Department in 1980 that their order for ship lumber was ready. To their confusion, they hadn't recalled ordering any ship lumber. They later discovered that in 1829, the Bishop of Strangnas had ordered that 20,000 oak trees be planted (on a specific island) and be protected for the Navy. It apparently takes oak trees 150-years to mature and anticipating a shortage of lumber at the turn of the twenty-first century (and believing that war supplies would probably still be needed), Strangnas ordered that the trees be planted and preserved.

That's some seriously long term thinking! While 150-years will not be the required investment in all of your life's endeavors, consider the legacy mindset here. Every action, every word spoken and every investment made into a relationship, business or career, is like a seed being planted that will ultimately multiply into a result similar to and greater than what was initially planted.

In this life, there are those willing to make the investment, and those who are not.

Which are you?

People. Passion. Profit.

Making a serious impact is one of the hardest things you do: You have to look into the soul of who you are, explore what really matters to you, and infuse that into every element of your work or daily hustle. In business, there is a term called a *triple bottom line,* which includes People, Planet and Profit, meaning that particular business positively impacts those three key areas. Servicing people in some way, being "green" or environmentally friendly, and making a profit. Your life's purpose also has a triple bottom line. I like to refer to it as People, Passion, and Profit. Your life's purpose will always involve service that increases or improves others' lives. It will most likely be in the lane of your greatest passion, interests or talent. And you will of course profit from what you're best at.

We are a generation determined to rewrite our destinies and outrun the *who* and *what* we are expected to be. And within these pages lies the formula:

STEP ONE: Identity

Identifying the labels and deconstructing the harmful and hurtful experiences that have been invited upon you (whether by adults or peers). The names or experiences that have damaged your self-esteem, negatively influenced your character, behavior and ultimately shaped how you might view yourself and others. We will then provide the essential building blocks to expose and expel those very influences that have pressured or convinced you to live inauthentically.

STEP TWO: Finding What Fits

We will do a deep internal dive to locate and activate on your individual talents and unchanging strengths. We'll explore how focusing on developing your core strengths will help you to have a lasting impact on the world and become the kind of individual that people can look up to.

STEP THREE: Execution

Obviously, none of this will mean anything without some straight up action! So lastly, we will unpack a duplicatable system of timeless success strategies to help you to achieve your goals (both big and small). We will cover a fast action plan around those goals that puts your strengths to action and places a demand on your courage, desire to do better, have better and be better.

UNFOLLOW

THE CROWD

My life is over

I knew for sure we would be arrested. Kicked out of school. Sued by the victim. And utterly shamed as we faced news cameras and classmates witnessing us being escorted across our campus in handcuffs. I could only imagine the headlines: *"Popular College Fraternity Threatens Fellow Student at Gunpoint"*.

I had just arrived back at my dorm room when I got the call, notifying me that a few of my fraternity brothers did "something stupid". Apparently some guy on campus was spotted wearing a t-shirt with my fraternity's letters and insignia. He was a non-member and wearing our paraphernalia. A privilege reserved for members-only and a supreme offense, punishable by a swift thrashing or worse (only in the fraternity world, of course). It was explained to me that this non-member was later cornered in a public restroom, threatened at gunpoint by "one of us" and had later decided to pursue the matter to the fullest extent of the law with the help of local police.

There was no hard evidence against us. No external witnesses. No "smoking gun". But I knew the story was true. We were the most popular group on campus out of 20-thousand students. Heads turned every time we walked into a room or stadium (literally). People from all over the state would travel the distance to try and get into one of our always packed out parties. We had it all. The "fame". The prestige. And EVERY guy wanted to be "one of us". Enough to risk wearing the "members-only" t-shirt for a momentary feeling of *belonging*. And I knew that minor offense was enough to make "one of us" get up and *do something* about it. After all. This wouldn't have been first time our *band of brotherhood* had done something less than smart.

There was the time when over 20 of us drove up the street to a neighboring college and engaged in a crowd fight with another fraternity. *Their* group had crashed a party of ours earlier that night and caused some trouble, forcing our event to be shut down. And this was our retaliation. And then there was the time when we drove two stretch Hummers across the school Presidents' front lawn while he was having his annual garden party fundraiser with several important investors (We were attempting a shortcut to avoid traffic).

(So back to the gun incident)

Why did we do it?

Well to be exact, *we* didn't! Only two of our fraternity members were being accused, and ironically those were the only two missing in attendance at the hearing the next morning, as I suspect they lacked the courage to show their faces. But this time we were all summoned for questioning and to pay the price. So there we sat, in the dean's office on a Saturday morning, shamefully facing the powers that be. We could have been expelled immediately, stripped of all fraternity privileges and lost everything. Even if this one incident wasn't sufficient for expulsion, we had already given them a track record of offenses. Plenty of motivation to do their worst.

Ultimately, the accuser had forgotten some key details regarding the incident. His story changed a few times and he was inconsistent. Therefore, no legal action taken against us. No arrests. No suspensions. We were released with zero punishment. We had gotten away with it.

I share this story with you as a *CAUTION*

You might be asking why? What would make someone do something so stupid? Thoughtless? Dangerous?

We did it because

We were afraid of losing the acceptance and approval of others. The older fraternity brothers who had blazed the trails long before us. They had dubbed us newer brothers with the nickname: *Chaotic.* And we paid the price for our membership and acceptance through a series of foolish choices in order to live up to a name that we had been given and were expected to carry out. An expected standard that we thought we had to live up to.

Our identity was handed to us. We were told who we were.

Here's the lesson: When you don't decide your identity for yourself, you will end up allowing someone else to decide it *for* you. And then you must continue to live up to the labels that you were given if you want to remain in their good graces. Even if the person you are morphing into is someone you don't recognize or like. That kind of existence is draining, costly and **absolutely NO way to live your life!** (More on this later)

Please ask yourself

How many times have you done something less than smart to please someone else or to earn their affections? How often have you stayed in a relationship that you knew was unhealthy? How many times have you allowed peer pressure to guide your choices? How many times have you chosen to not stand up for yourself when you should have, because you were afraid of losing the affections of those whom you sought to please? How often have you competed or pursued a goal because in the end it would make you feel valuable, respected or simply accepted by others? How often have you silenced your inner voice that was begging you to recognize and avoid the danger ahead?

Here's some truth: We have all done it. Myself included. But why do we do it?

If we're being honest

The *why* is always simple: Because at the very core of our very humanity, we desire validation. We desire acceptance. Compassion. To feel important. Respected. Powerful. To be treated by others with the same love that we feel for ourselves. Buried in the deepest centers of our goals and pursuits is a <u>feeling</u> that tugs at our emotions and pulls on our heartstrings. It is those emotions that most often control our everyday choices. And usually cause us to pursue the wrong goals in life.

That's why *we* did it. That's why we joined *the fraternity*

Because of everything that it would mean for our egos. We did it to feel important. We did it for the prestige. The attention. The feeling of power. Popularity. The respect of the crowd. Each of us felt the urge and temptation to be a part of the "group". It was something bigger than us that would help us to feel as important as we deeply wanted to be. Out of 850 applicants - they chose *us*. And the pressure was on. And of course we were involved in community service projects, mentoring in schools and feeding the homeless, serving in soup kitchens when we were required to. But let's be honest, we didn't know who we were yet. We did it for the "fame".

Validation. We all want it. We look for it everywhere: Family, friends, jobs, and it's never enough. It's a bottomless pit and our egos thrive on it. Enter the world of social media, which is one of the best dopamine producing, validation centers that we can access immediately – right next to drugs and alcohol. Let me be clear. There is nothing wrong with social media (I built an entire business from it). What's dangerous, however, is the imbalance of its usage. When we have allowed it to control our emotional thermostat, then there is an imbalance. Let's fuse this idea with present day circumstances. We have more opportunities than ever for validation, which only feeds the addiction:

The number of *hearts* or *likes* we get on a post.

The number of *followers* or *subscribers* on a social media channel.

The number of *compliments* we receive on any given day.

If we are not careful to avoid validation slavery, we will end up allowing our validators dictate the choices we make, even though they aren't the ones who will live with the outcomes of our decisions. We will end up following a script. A course of living in service to the people who we will never be good enough for, as opposed to the people who may be rooting for us.

Let me be even clearer. Social media is not the drug. The craving for validation is. The more we depend on it, the higher dosage of it we we'll need for it to work. And when it's gone, we'll experience everything that we would with drug withdrawal – darkness, loss, pain, and the unquenchable desire for more.

I have a better idea. Chase purpose instead of validation. I agree that it's a radical idea, but at the end of the day, that's really what we want anyway right? To be really truly happy. Fulfilled. To know that we're making a real difference and impact wherever we find ourselves. At school. On the job. In our relationships. That's how you live. Within these pages is the chance to explore what that means for you, along with exercises, relevant stories, activities and some straight up wisdom to help you identify your own unique value that you might bring to the world and building blocks to discover the impact that you could make. Focusing on purpose gives us power over the things that we can control.

So I have a friend…

Sean and I were hanging out one afternoon. The weather was a perfect 70-degrees and sunny in my home state of Florida. Sean was quieter than normal that day and apparently had something on his mind. So I inquired. He had just received a promotion and raise at work yet he was unsatisfied with his current career status. He had received a generous increase in pay, title and responsibility. But it wasn't enough. This job wasn't where he truly wanted to be. So I asked the obvious question. "What would you rather be doing instead?" Sean shared with me, in his most genuine tone, that he wouldn't be satisfied until he achieved his goal of living at 1600 Pennsylvania Avenue. I paused in a bit of confusion. "The White House?" I asked. Still suspended in that moment of confusion, I asked, "Why do you want to live at the White House"? Then it hit me. "Oh! You want to be… the *President?!*" I said. He nodded.

So here's the thing

We all have goals. And I believe that anything we dare to put our minds, hearts and intentions to, have a great chance of becoming possible. But I also believe that we have an even greater responsibility to be honest with ourselves regarding our true intentions. So allow me to elaborate further on the opening question in the introduction (*Why aren't we famous yet?*). Please see my personal definition of "famous" below:

Famous: Popular, powerful, respected, accepted, validated, in control, cherished, celebrated by others, to feel larger than life (and any other emotional trigger-word you can think of that resonates with your need for internal fulfillment).

So why aren't we "famous" yet? Because in most cases, we are after the wrong goals. I have often found that we select careers or goals because of what we believe the fancy title or achievement will do for us emotionally. Please learn from my earlier story. "Fame", popularity or living in the spotlight will not fix you, bring you fulfillment or resolve your emotional issues. It only introduces more issues if you are not in goal pursuit for the right reasons.

Ask yourself: Why is *this* goal so important to me? How will I *feel* when I achieve this goal (besides *accomplished*)? Maybe becoming the leader of the Free World isn't your goal. Maybe your goal is to become class president, to win an award, or to get into a certain college. Whatever that goal is, be honest and ask yourself: What will attaining this goal actually do for me? How will I *feel* when I arrive? By the way, *"happy"* is not a sufficient answer! Go deeper. Will you feel important? Will you feel fulfilled? Then answer the question: *why will having this goal make me feel that way?*

My goal is to: _____

Achieving this goal will make me *feel*: _____

Why I will feel this way: _____

PROVE THAT YOUR GOALS ARE REAL THROUGH ACTIONS AND DEEDS

Note: We all want the "white picket fence" but how many of us are willing to go get the paint, give up a weekend and earn a few blisters?

If your goal is genuine. If your goal really means the world to you, then there should be a very real trail of evidence behind you of *actions taken* in the direction of your goal (especially if you want people to truly believe that your goal is anything more than an ego-trip). True goals always involve people who stand to benefit (along the way) as a result of you having achieved them. There is no such thing as: 'One day' I'll be able help people *after* I've made enough money. *After* I'm finished with school. *After* I get the job. There is *always* something you can be doing right now! You can take on a (lower level) part time job in your field of interest. You can volunteer your time. You can read up on that career and share your knowledge with others. Your passion for your future achieved goal should rub off on people. It should be *evident*. If there is no road paved behind you in the form of your footprints, then roll up your sleeves and begin paving!

But before you do, ask yourself: Who do I want to serve in the world? What impact do I want to make? What specific areas of humanity do I want to affect? Truthfully, most of us are more likely to gravitate towards the thing with the shiny title that we believe will make us *look* good or feel good. Is your reason heartfelt? Please understand that anytime you choose the path to success, there will be much resistance and many challenges ahead. Is your reason for going after this goal strong enough to pull you forward when the road gets tough?

Your *why* matters

The best "why" is the one that serves the people in your world and the greater good. Your "why" should be connected to something in your heart and soul that you just cannot ignore. Your "why" should contain an identifiable human need that you feel you <u>must</u> do something about. It should involve some sector of the world where you can see your passion, talents and abilities being a fit. And above all it MUST be a reason beyond egotistical self-service. Otherwise, attaining that goal will be dangerous. In the sense that it will not bring you the happiness or fulfillment that you crave, as much as it will introduce to you a whole new level of problems to deal with.

So here's the TRUTH

You (the one reading this) are the most important person alive, because NO ONE ELSE has what you have. No one is as unique as you. No one else has your story. No one else has your combination of passion, looks, background, strengths, weaknesses, thoughts, likes, personality, skills, hot buttons, experiences, purpose or path in life. You are the only *you* in existence and there will never be another *you* ever again! There is an entire world out there waiting for <u>you</u> to show up and show us all who you *are*. Don't waste that opportunity chasing after cheap external validations. Your ego is NOT your friend.

It all boils down to this

This is not about upstaging the person sitting next to you. It's not about being better than someone else or finishing the race first. It's not about "fame" (the emotional gaps that your ego seeks to fill). It's not even about *smarts*. It's about deciding *who you are* and standing firm in your resolve! Refusing to allow someone else to craft your identity for you. It's about making one wise choice with your life, over and over. Choices that will most often challenge the ego but serve the greater good and humanity. It is about becoming the YOU that doesn't bend your moral standards for the benefit of attention or external validation. It is being surefooted in your purpose.

In a world full of people who are giving up their individuality to imitate the status quo or whatever our pop-culture calls *cool, hot* or *acceptable*; what the world really needs is for you to be your original and authentic self! The world needs you to make your personal mark and leave a unique footprint that no one else can fill. That's a tall order, but it's a job that only you can do. I will argue that your most important assignment while we're spinning around this *rock* (Earth), is to define who you are for yourself, what you're supposed to be doing while you're here and get moving! The entire world is waiting to see who you will choose to become. That little reality should mean EVERYTHING to you! Don't you dare leave this world without leaving your footprint!

Somewhere between your real dreams and your reality, is your choice about what kind of story you will live and how you will live it. The world already has more than enough people who are settling for "average". Colleges are pumping out thousands of them every year and we're running out of spaces to employ them all. I want you to become the courageous, unique, no-B.S version of yourself that the world is waiting to see. Within these pages is your chance to find it. Own it. Do It. And show the world who you really are!

Let's get to work!

THE
MILLENNIAL
ISSUE

Growing up, I was always taught that if I wanted to be successful, happy, and avoid failure, that I needed to:

1. Go to school

And…

2. Get *really* good grades

… And as long as I did these two things I could earn a scholarship to attend a *really good* college. But it doesn't end there. Once in college I then had to repeat the cycle. Which meant: Study even harder and get better grades so that at the end of four years I could graduate and land a *really good* job! Essentially, this was the script that had been written for my life: A. Work hard B. Get a job C. Keep a job D. Retire in thirty-five years and have a nice life. Happy trails!

So I followed "the plan". I worked hard in school, graduated with superior honors and still wound up jobless. Without the one thing promised to me at the end of the college journey. I found out that the greatest common hurt of successful college grads, is to bury their hearts and dreams in order to follow "the plan", trusting the process and often feeling as if life cheated them in the end. Ultimately entering into a cold and uncaring world with a broken heart and resenting the journey.

- *"Most people die at 21. We just don't bury them until they are 65." - Benjamin Franklin*

Most students graduate college somewhere north of 21-years of age. If lucky, they land a job, although it's usually not the job they want, but because they need the job, they take the job. They usually haul themselves out of bed each morning, 'clock-in', make average money (which is just about enough to eat, split rent with a roommate and pay a cell phone bill) and cannot wait for the two-day weekend to arrive (wash and repeat). I starting thinking, 'how miserable is that'? There had to be more to life than merely working and just "getting by". What about being *happy*, doing what you *love* and never having to worry about *money*? Where are the college classes for *that*? Was this supposed "good-life" reserved only for a select group of "lucky" people who had been fortunate enough to drink from the proverbial "fountain of good fortune"?

Become a Kid Again: The amazing 5-year old

Let's rewind. Do you remember that amazing 5-year old that you used to be? That time in life when your imagination could make you believe that anything was possible? Where one day you imagined that you would become an astronaut, a fireman, a ballerina (or even a superhero). Those times in your life where you would stand at the top of the stairs and wrap a blanket around your neck, pretending that it gave you Superman powers and dared to believe that just maybe you could fly if you took 'the leap' and concentrated hard enough on the way down. That any fantastical impossibilities could actually become your reality if you had the audacity to 'believe'.

What happened to *THAT* person?

In the illustration, you will see what looks to be an ordinary glass jar, but today it is going to double as a *flea trap*. Catching fleas in a jar was a popular activity for many kids growing up. One would go into a grassy or wooded area, find jumping fleas and trap them in a jar. The problem with this was that they could easily jump out and escape. So in order to keep the fleas from jumping out, you would have to place a piece of cardboard or some sort of barrier over the top of the jar for about an hour (give or take).

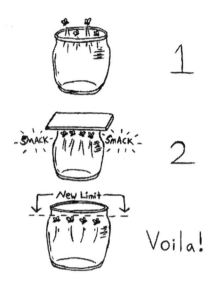

During that hour, the fleas inside would jump in an attempt to escape, but would end up "smacking their heads" against the barrier at the top of the jar. After the hour is up, you would return to the jar and remove the piece of cardboard barrier, and although the fleas would still maintain the physical ability to jump out of the jar, something had changed. The fleas would now jump no higher than the cardboard barrier that was once there. They have effectively been trained to go no higher than their newly perceived limitations. In the human world, this is a mindset that I call *average*.

Over time, as we are growing up, we tend to lose the imaginative and childlike essence of dreaming as we are told things like: '*Get your head out of the clouds. Sit down. Be quiet. Don't talk. That's unrealistic. Color inside the lines. Put that down. You're not talented enough or good enough or don't have high enough test scores. That's ridiculous. You should really come up with a plan-B*'. After we spend enough time "smacking our heads" against these proverbial "barriers" we tend start believing that the dreams we once had or should have are unrealistic and even worse, that we lack the capacity to achieve them. We have officially been *programmed.*

Have you become *that person*?

The person you promised yourself that you would never turn into? The jerk? The depressed person on your way to pursuing a major or a career that you never wanted? Or maybe you're just settling for *average*. If so, consider the possibility that that's not who you originally wanted to be. I want to you to go back to the time when you thought anything was possible. When you had dreams of making your mark in the universe or just doing something that you would absolutely love. Connect again with what your dreams were. When you first jumped up and decided: '*I want to change the world*'. Ask yourself right now: What is the difference I want to make in the world I live in and why? That's the *real* you. Not the expected standard that many people have chosen to live.

Note: The "expected standard" is the life you lead when you do only what's expected of you. It is "the script" that has been written for you. But it is usually way beneath the level of your real potential and places zero demand on your dreams, talents or true strengths. It is most often boring, without color or life and it certainly didn't consult you in the planning process. You do not have to be the "expected standard".

The "Butterfly Effect"

So we did this cool biology project in the 3rd grade where we got to "grow" butterflies. It began with all of us kids going outside and catching caterpillars, building individual nest boxes constructed from popsicle sticks and filled with grass. The captured caterpillar ultimately encloses itself in a self-made cocoon and then comes the wait. At the end of its metamorphosis of transforming into a butterfly, there is a final hatching process that must be free from human intervention. After weeks of waiting, an energetic group of twenty-seven 3rd graders would rush over to the classroom biology corner at the first sign of the hatching cocoons. Because the actual hatching process can take several minutes (and small children can be a bit impatient) the first thing we wanted to do was "assist" for fear that they would be stuck in the cocoon and wouldn't make it out (or just sheer impatience). Big mistake. The process of a butterfly hatching from its cocoon involves pressing its wings against the shell in order to break out. A sequence that promotes blood flow, providing essential wing strength if the butterfly will ever hope to take flight. Disrupting this process results in them being weak, without ever taking flight.

The Millennial Issue

Think about how this "Butterfly Effect" relates to modern day life. We, the current generation, are often the unfortunate victims of some well-intended, yet failed parenting strategies that have played a role in making our generation weaker. As an example, many of us were told that we could have anything we wanted, just because we wanted it. Many of us were told that we were special (all the time) breaking our way into honors classes, skipping grades, landing A's and earning trophy's (or participation awards) not always because we deserved it, but because some of our parents complained or fought to get us things that we had not earned on our own sweat and competence.

So then, we graduate school, get thrust into the real world and almost instantly we find out that the world doesn't perceive us to be as special as we were told. Our parents can't get us promotions by complaining to our bosses and we certainly get no rewards for coming in last. A perfect storm for a completely shattered self-image. And if we are lucky enough to land jobs, in an oversaturated market that is pumping out college grads faster than we can employ them, we are faced with a few other challenges:

Lazy.

Entitled.

Apathetic.

Spoiled.

Impatient.

"Disruptors" who are difficult to work with.

… Just a few of the many indictments our Millennial generation is slapped with. Not to mention being tough for employers to manage.

But I want MORE

What all of us really want is to feel a sense of purpose and fulfillment (especially at work). We want coaches, not bosses and dictators. Those who are interested in developing our truest of strengths. We want a life of meaning, clarity and to know that we are succeeding at making a difference. But too often, we graduate and find ourselves in organizations with little interest in our innate talents, proclivities, or personal development and often fail to see the difference we are making, if any.

Some of us more radical "Disruptors" desiring change often rebel against the institution and demand that the powers that be perform hygiene or simply eliminate long established or antiquated management processes and ways of conducting business. Too often we look for our bosses or leaders to change their leadership styles to conform to our development needs.

Here's the truth

Your job can only take you so far. Even if you do manage to ignite change (at the school you attend or at your workplace), or if your employer decides to offer some kickbacks, awards more vacation days, quarterly bonuses, expense paid retreats, beanbag chairs and free snacks, there will inevitably come a point where nothing they can do will make you happy *enough*. You will still want *more*.

So let's say you've worked hard and managed to land a job, but it's not *enough*. You've made some impact, but it's not *enough*. You earned several raises as a nod to your hardest efforts, and still, it isn't *enough*. The true satisfaction and payout *feeling* isn't there. You want more than what is being offered to you. That much is understood, but where most people struggle is in being able to clearly define what that *more* actually is.

A job, even if it's the perfect fit and in the vein of your core passion and talents, is still paying you to achieve *their* corporate purpose, not your own. And your personal purpose is really what you have been craving. It's that place of true fulfillment where your unique combination of talents, personality, experience and strengths align with opportunities to create an impact. It's what speaks to you and feeds your soul. We look for it in everything we do and are never satisfied until we find it.

We don't just want our *work* to matter. We don't just want what we *do* to matter. *We* want to matter. There will come a day, where despite how much money you are making or how much fun you are having at work, you will find yourself wanting *more*. A life beyond the written script and the expected standard. A life full of meaning, adventure and purpose that is custom fit for you. We expect these very institutions (whether they be our school or employer) to supply us with purpose, meaning, and specialized work that impacts the world on a greater scale.

So rather than wasting your time rebelling against the institution or expecting others to change and conform, I believe there is a better use for your energy and effort. We misalign our expectations when we find ourselves demanding that employers recognize, develop and award us on our talents and strengths, and vision cast our "yellow-brick-road" to happiness when we have failed to clearly define what those things actually are for ourselves.

Hence the age old question: *Where do you see yourself in 10-years?* And by the way, *"happy and making a lot of money"* is not a clear answer. What are you best at? What people in the world do you see yourself serving? What are your core strengths? What kind of work do you love doing so much that you would do it for free, but plan to specialize in so that you can get paid for it? We need to be vividly clear on what that picture looks like (for ourselves) before we can pursue it, let alone expect anyone else to provide it for us.

"I have a dream!"... Do you really?

If you have a dream. Something that you really want out of life. Then take some action! Think of at least one thing that you can be doing about that dream today and get moving. What delays dream fulfillment is when we sit back and wait for people to come along and help, when in reality people don't come along to help until they first see you moving, investing, risking and commit to having your own 'skin in the game'. As long as you're sitting still doing nothing, no one is coming to your aid. There will never be anyone that feels sorry enough for you to just hand you the big break that you've been hoping for.

The kinds of people that get the big breaks in life are the ones that are out there doing something about their dreams. The ones who are sacrificing sleep. The ones who believe in their dream so much that they aren't wasting time feeling sorry for themselves or afraid to take 'the leap'. Okay, so maybe you tried once or twice and it didn't work out. Maybe you put everything on the line. Your pride. Your money. Everything. Maybe you crashed and burned. Maybe you were embarrassed. Maybe everyone talked about you. Maybe you decided that you would never take a risk like that ever again.

I'll concede with you for a moment. Yes, it can be painful. Similar to working out for the first time. You may go into the gym and bench press 150-pounds. You'll probably wake up the next morning with sore muscles, feeling like you have a charlie horse in your chest and arms and in the most pain you've ever felt in your life.

We have all felt this gloriously painful growth, especially if we didn't 'win the prize', place first in the competition or receive noticeable returns on all of our hard work. Get back up and keep moving. What did you learn? Do it differently this next time around. Ask better questions. Make it better. Keep it moving. Work smarter. Try it again and again. Do it differently until you get different results. True winners aren't afraid of failing a few times before a win actually happens. You are only a failure when you decide to stop trying. Putting everything on the line is usually what life will require from us. Especially when what we want is valuable. Get used to it. That's the cost of pursuing your dreams and it must be worth it to you.

But no one believes in me

Not true. But I know the feeling! Consider this. We all have people in our lives who don't believe in our dreams. And that's actually the way it is supposed to be! Oftentimes we press 'pause' on our lives because we are waiting on people to believe in us, support us and be our cheerleaders. We're waiting on them to give us the energy and wherewithal to take action. But that energy must come from *you*.

Others are not required to believe in your dream because they were not given the dream. You were. The dreamer is the one responsible for motivating others to believe in the dream. Not the other way around. Other people will believe in your dreams when they see you taking fervent action. Then it's real! They are waiting to see how badly you want it before they come aboard with their investment. Others will believe in you if you don't quit.

My parents

My parents are people that I respect more than anyone. They are great people whom everyone loves and looks up to. They are respectable, loving, and popular, but I saw how hard they labored for their income. Their jobs were stressful and they never talked about *loving* their work. I only remember them leaving the house in the morning, where they would go into a building for eight-hours out of the day, and then came home drained and exhausted. I loved them, but I just didn't want to "be like them" in that regard. Even at a very young I knew that I wanted to *love* my life. Just being content and comfortable was not enough. I was convinced that real happiness was out there and available, so I decided that no matter what it would take, I was going to live a life of happiness. And I'm sure that on some level, you want that as well.

In my mind, there is nothing more depressing than walking through life without actually *living.* After careful research, I found out that depressed people of all ages are four times more likely to have a heart attack in the next fourteen-years as opposed to those who are truly happy. I found out that a vast majority of people in the workforce hate their jobs, are broke, unhappy, contract more diseases and die earlier. There is nothing fun or admirable about being *average,* and something tells me, *you too* want better for yourself, like I did. Something tells me that you want the best shot you have at a life full of happiness and fulfillment.

Note: If you do not wake up every morning *loving your life….* then there is a problem.

Anatomy lesson: When we are happy, laughing, and finding enjoyment in something, endorphins (also known as the "happy" chemical) are released through the brain, causing us to feel a sense of euphoria, energy and peace. It's like a dose of healthy medicine in the body that scientifically helps us to live longer. On the contrary, depression, anger and sadness slowly *kills* us. It increases your risk of a number of diseases and other conditions by, for example, increasing levels of stress hormones such as cortisol or adrenaline. It affects the immune system, making it harder for your body to fight infection, heart disease and an increased risk for substance abuse.

My point: We human beings do not have bodies that are physically designed to sustain depression and unhappiness. **All of this to say:** Don't be satisfied with *average. You* are physically designed to be happy and enjoy your life!

Come to life!

As a kid I've always loved to read out loud in class. I loved Spelling, English, Speech and everything about the subjects. In grade school, my favorite moments were when the teacher would ask someone to volunteer to stand up and read aloud. I was always the first one to volunteer and anytime there came an opportunity to speak publicly or read aloud I jumped at the chance.

I didn't know why I loved to write, read and speak out loud. I only knew that I felt this amazing rush of energy throughout my body anytime I got the chance to do so. It was my favorite part of class and something that I always looked forward to. To me, it didn't matter that I was <u>not</u> the best at it or that I never made it past round-two at our school Spelling Bees. All I wanted was the chance to be involved; the chance to exercise the thing <u>that I loved to do the most</u>. On some level, I'm sure you feel the same way about the things that you love.

A life altering day

When I was in the 6th grade, one of my teachers took our classroom on a field trip to a local news station, where me and all of my peers got to sit inside of an NBC affiliate studio and witness a live newscast taping. As I watched the two anchors at the news desk read stories and share information with the public, something inside of me '<u>came alive</u>'. All of a sudden, while watching the news anchors perform their craft, I had the greatest moment of realization of my entire life: '<u>That</u> is what I want to <u>be</u> when I grow up'! What more perfect job to have, that would utilize my unique combination of passions, talents, strengths, abilities and actually <u>pay</u> me for it!

I had <u>found</u> the place that would allow me to use my love for writing and reading aloud, that would afford me a lifestyle I would enjoy while I could share my gifts with the world. It was the biggest rush I had ever felt! I was in 'Heaven'. This is where I fit! This is what I was born to do! I had found the 'thing' that I knew I would be doing for the rest of my life!

It's like discovering your "powers" for the first time

In the 2013 movie reprise, *Man of Steel (Superman),* we witness the young Clark Kent on a normal sunny afternoon, running through a series of farm fields at warp speeds, having the time of his life, as he jumps over seventy-feet in the air with hang times that were nothing short of supernatural. On the last jump, however, he became a bit overzealous, trips and was about to smack head-first into the ground. Fearing for his life, he covers his face with his arms at the fear of a crash-landing. The intense musical climax of the scene prepared movie viewers to expect the worse, and right at the moment that we all thought he would meet his fate… No crash. No big bang. Only silence. Seconds later, we watch young Clark as he slowly opens his eyes to find himself floating in midair, parallel to the grounds' dirt and gravel, just inches beneath him. He had discovered for the first time that he had the power to fly.

There is a visceral feeling that we get when we are fully operating in the *stuff* that we feel we were meant to do. That place where our perfect blend of talents, strengths, passion and the right situation, all merge. Sometimes in life, you won't come to discover your full range of abilities until you face a pressure laden situation where the need for survival is your only option; those moments where every ounce of your energy, brain power and ability all come to the surface in full force to execute victory.

If you would only <u>commit</u>!

We have all heard the extraordinary stories about panicked individuals who have managed to access superhuman strength in life threatening situations. One such occasion, was 2013, in Oregon, when teenage sisters, Hanna (age 16) and Haylee (age 14) together, lifted an entire tractor to save their father who was pinned underneath. To them, it made no difference whether or not they possessed the physical capacity to achieve the task. They <u>committed</u>! And as they did, their 'super powers' showed up!

Advanced brain and anatomy research reveals something quite fascinating about human beings possessing "hidden superpowers". Recent studies have discovered that the human brain's automatic fear-response systems can cause human beings to unleash hidden mental and physical abilities when under extreme circumstances and life threatening situations; causing one to have some accesses their 'absolute power level', all depending of course on their <u>level of commitment</u>.

Note: What these stories reveal to us is the mystery of all human potential, and that is this: When we decide and _fully commit_ ourselves to doing something, we nearly become an unstoppable force! When is the last time you <u>fully committed</u> yourself?

Consider this: That same kind of superhuman 'power' resides in _you_ as well! I am convinced that even in the most painful, intense and dire life situations that you will ever face, _you_ are already equipped with all of the physical and mental potential that you need in order to succeed over adversity, live out your dreams and achieve _anything_ that you are <u>willing</u> to truly commit yourself to. Have _you_ discovered your powers yet?

Don't Die Young

You only die when you give up on the belief that your potential has value. When you are afraid to try because the effort might cause you a little pain. Because of the sacrifice or inconvenience that it may require. You die young when you refuse to take a chance on your potential for fear that it may not work on the first attempt. To be fully aware that you could actually achieve your dreams but refuse to take a step because you're afraid of a little training, inconvenience or competition. To fear the person that you might have to become in order to have what you've always dreamed of having.

To tell yourself: _"I could probably have that dream or become that phenomenal person I want to be. But because I've been taught to sit down, color within the lines, that real success is reserved only for a fortunate few and to come up with a Plan-B… I'm imperfect anyway and I've made too many mistakes already. So why even bother? I'll probably fail. Or something will probably go wrong. So let's not endure the pain, or waste the money. Let's just do Plan-B and stay safe."_

Don't die young!

Take The Leap.

Ultimately, I encourage you to reconnect with that inner 5-year old. The one who taught you how to dream. The person you were before you got your head "smacked" one too many times. That brutally honest, no B-S, courageous, cute, crazy, ambitious little artist of a human being that taught you how to walk, talk and deal with the world. The one who taught you how to love yourself (and didn't mind screaming it from the rooftops). The one who wasn't afraid to fail and try again. The one who wasn't afraid to run, trip and fall (and possibly break something) to then get back up and try again. The one who wasn't afraid to be his or herself regardless of what anyone else thought about them. Somewhere along the way we lose that inner 5-year old and the challenge becomes getting them back.

That inner 5-year old holds the clues to everything you ever thought possible for your future. As you venture through these pages, I want you to decide who it is that you want to be. And take a chance on that person. The one you always wanted to be. The version of yourself that will require some training, grooming and hard work to become. That person that's going to do something to better the world, get paid for it and actually be happy doing it. Even if you don't know what it is yet. That is the real you. That's the person you are supposed to become. That's where the real happiness and payoff in life is. That inner 5-year old is begging you to just take a chance on the fact that your dreams are actually real. That you could actually become the person you always wanted to be. That 'the leap' could actually be worth the risk required.

Homework:

The solution to achieving the things we really want, even after life has fooled us into believing that we cannot have them, is belief + deliberate, determined and consistent action = goal achievement!

I want you to reconnect with your truest dreams, desires or goals that are in your heart and mind, and write them down. Next, imagine five gutsy, yet realistic things that you can do this week, to either achieve or bring you closer to achieving that dream or goal. And then write them down. Because the truth is, brave action in spite of your fears or doubts, is the ONLY thing that is going to get you closer to your goal. Take your five action steps seriously, and do them!

Next, write down your WHY I will argue that your WHY is the most important part of the equation. Without knowing your personal purpose and desire behind your goal, you will have no energy to "pull you forward" when it gets tough or when you experience a setback. So you must know your WHY and it has to be strong! The best WHY is the one that serves the people in your world and the greater good. Your WHY should be connected to something in your heart and soul that you just cannot ignore. It should contain an identifiable human need that you feel you must do something about. It should involve some sector of the world where you can see your passion, talents and abilities being a t. And above all it MUST be a reason beyond egotistical self-service. Otherwise, attaining that goal will be dangerous. In the sense that it will not bring you the happiness or fulfillment that you crave, as much as it will introduce to you a whole new level of problems to deal with.

Lastly, I want you to write down how achieving that dream or goal will make you FEEL. Here's the thing: Goals and dreams must be attached to a feeling. They must resonate with you if you stand any chance of pushing through the tough times when it looks like your goals may not get done. The feelings that are attached to your goal achievement must be just as strong, if not stronger than your WHY.

When you write down the feeling attached to the goal, don't just say: "Achieving this goal will make me feel accomplished (or successful)". Dig deeper! That's where the good stuff is! Sometimes you may even discover that your motivation for going after the goal was out of nothing more than competitive jealousy over someone else (which is never a good reason to pursue a goal).

I would really like to _____

I have a dream of doing _____

I have a dream of becoming _____

I would like to try _____

Five brave things that I can do to achieve or bring myself closer to this dream / desire or goal:

A:_____

B:_____

C:_____

D:_____

E:_____

My "WHY":

_____

_____

_____

_____

_____

How achieving this goal will make me feel: _____

_____

ARE YOU IN THE RIGHT LANE?

EVERYONE has their own "lane" of genius

Genius: Someone who sees a target that no one else see's, and hits it!

I've always been passionate about finding your "lane" in life. Doing the things that make you come alive. The stuff that comes natural and makes the time go by. The stuff that others recognize you for being one of the best at doing. The stuff you do that makes other people think that you are a genius (when really you're just operating in your strengths). The stuff that leaves you feeling most fulfilled (whether you're paid for it or not). Chances are, you are already doing *it* without realizing it! Many a wise individual have quoted this age old quote: "When purpose and passion meet, you will never work another day in your life".

If you can manage to arrive at those crossroads, everything you feel you were ever meant to do in life starts happening. What results is a visceral feeling of happiness that is indescribable! Many will describe it as end epiphany, an overwhelming feeling of euphoria, but ultimately, it's just an experience that sadly too few of us manage to arrive at although every one of us *feels* we are supposed to have it.

At these crossroads, depression, sadness, suicidal thoughts, failure, even your painful past, will not stand a chance at survival. You will no longer depend on something else or someone else to make you happy or satisfied. These crossroads provide you a powerful glimpse of your future, your place in the world, the work that you must do, and a blissful happiness at the thought of achieving your dreams by doing what you love.

Self-Love

Too often, we evaluate our worth and value based on our connections. Who we're friends with. Who we're dating. What circles we run-in and who we hang out with. There's a certain inner-peace in falling in love with yourself because when you when you truly love yourself, you aren't worried about who else is going to love or accept you. You will then find more things to love about yourself and eventually you will look up and someone else is curious, because you've fallen in love with yourself and they are curious to fall in love with the authentic version of you too. But when you're afraid that moment won't ever come, you end up looking to fill your life with people instead of purpose. People who will require you to become something else to fit in their circle.

A little note regarding being happy: Sometimes we foolishly choose to use other people as our source of happiness in life; a girlfriend/boyfriend or a group of friends that we depend on to make us happy or feel good. Placing your hopes and expectations in other people to make you happy is a junk bond investment. People are only human and have more than the capacity to disappoint you, hurt you, abuse and let you down. It is a part of human nature.

In this lifetime, the best possible hope that you have at true happiness is to find out who you are, what you do best, and get moving (this book is full of activities that will help you to arrive at that point! Just keep reading). Investing this time in yourself will result in an indestructible, endless reserve of internal revenue that will pay you back every day for the rest of your life! And with so many negative messages in our world, online and in media about *who* you should be and *how* you should be, you had better know who you *are* or else the world will decide *for* you! Getting in your "lane" and staying there is the real solution to resolving depression, achieving real happiness, and creating a tangible lifelong legacy and protecting it!

Here's a little proof:

Comedian, Jim Carrey, is mentioned as being one of the biggest actors in Hollywood and is most well-known for his high energy slapstick comedy, arguably making him one of the funniest comedians on the planet (you've probably seen him in a movie or two).

In a keynote speech that aired on live television, he reflected (on his time, here on this planet) and realized that throughout his entire life he had always been "two people". On one hand, growing up, he was the "kid in the living-room being a 'monkey' and entertaining company", and then finding himself in another room trying to relieve his mother who was suffering from several illnesses from arthritis to depression and as he calls it, 'everything else in-between'.

Out of sheer love and belief that his mother's life meant something, he wanted her to be free from her pain and suffering. In his words, because she had given birth to someone who was worth something, her life was in turn *worth* something. Even as a small kid, he would sit in his bedroom with a legal pad and meditate, trying to figure out the meaning behind the looming questions: *Why am I here?* And *what is life was all about?* Questions that we all at some point will ask.

The Million-Dollar Answer

One day, Carrey came across an ancient proverb (from Buddha) that stated: *"The true meaning of life is indeed about relieving suffering"*. It was then that he realized that his gift to produce laughter was making people feel better. Just by being his natural and authentic *self,* he was bringing healing to people by alleviating pain, all through the power of laughter. Upon this realization, Carrey recalls feeling like the luckiest person on earth. He had found his own answer to the million-dollar questions: *Why am I here? and what in the world am I supposed to be doing with my life?*

In that one moment, he had managed to bridge the connection between talent, passion, those he was supposed to service in life and the results he could produce. We can wrap this life journey of a successful star into a priceless package called *purpose.* Sure, one might argue: *well aren't there thousands of comedians on the planet? Does this mean that they all service the same needs and problems in the world?* Not necessarily. Consider the fact that not every funny person that tells jokes has the ability to make everyone laugh.

There are some comedians who do well with one type of audience while others excel in a different crowd of people. Quite frankly, there are a few comedians that I enjoy and others that don't make me laugh at all (even though they are famous). My point is, there is plenty of room for *everyone,* plenty of work to be done (enough for everyone to exercise and be rewarded for their authenticity), and more than enough people on the planet to serve. All through exercising the personal strengths that come natural to you.

Have you been *discovered* yet?

If you can manage to pair what *you* do *best,* combined with passion, the people that benefit from your talents, gifts and the results that they produce, you too will come to experience that visceral feeling of true fulfillment. Looking at it this way takes you away from being competitive with other people who may also excel in your category of talents. This mindset puts you in a lane all by yourself even when there are people out there who you may think do what you do better. Achievement is not necessarily about competing and winning against someone else. It's about bringing the absolute best of your genuine and authentic *self* to the surface, and then having the courage to show up in the world and actually put your strengths to work so that humanity can benefit.

While we're on this topic, I want you to begin to ponder on your passions, your talents and the very things that make *you* unique. What is your dream in life? What do you see yourself doing in your near future? Before the year is over? What kinds of people do you see yourself serving later in life? Where do you see yourself living? What is your *real* passion? I am not asking you to have your entire life figured out *today,* but if you could do anything in the world, what kind of work would you be doing and what kinds of results do you imagine this producing? What do you believe that you are most passionate about that you would not mind waking up every single day to do? What one thing do you love so much that you would you do for free?

Just as an exercise, write it down here:

(*What I do best is*):

_____

_____

_____

_____

_____

_____

(What kinds of people in the world will most benefit from what I do best?)

_____

_____

_____

_____

_____

_____

Ultimately, the goal is to learn how to do what it is that you're passion about, so well in fact, that you ultimately get paid untold amounts of money for it, all while using that gift to make a difference in the world.

I want to caution you, however. It is in our very human nature to compare ourselves to other well-known people in the world whom we believe to be *better at it* than we currently are. I call this period, our "unproven" stage. It's when we are in the process of figuring out who we are, where we belong and are working on our talents, but just can't help but get frustrated over the inevitable *self*-compare. This is where we fall for believing that we aren't tall enough, good looking enough, old enough, young enough, have enough money, friends or connections, smart enough, talented enough or talented at all. As we will discuss later, these are all little lies that pop up in our heads to try and get us to quit and refuse to try again. What will ultimately happen, if not careful, is we will slowly start to give up on the hope of every being able rise to the heights of those that are professionals in our category.

Note: No one ever won anything or arrived at an achieved goal by quitting.

Them VS. You

Do you have someone in mind who *does it better* than you? Well here is my advice:

I say, rather than studying that individuals' <u>current</u> success, go and study their beginnings! Go online and see if you can find some early video footage of when they were first starting out in their careers. You may just find out that where they started is very comparable to where you are currently. What's more important than where they are is where they <u>started</u>. Jim Carrey, over time, with passion and persistence, ultimately became the *new standard* of comedian.

If you are alive and living on this earth, I will argue that there is room for you to rise to the top of your game. The thing is, we have this little human tendency to believe that those who succeed have a special *something* that we just don't have. Something that they were born with that we can't learn or access. Sure the person you admire may be talented, accomplished and confident. But I'm willing to bet they weren't always like this. They probably started out a little fearful, uncertain and faced all of the same questions we all face: *Am I good enough? Am I talented enough? Am I smart enough?* You fill in the rest.

You will always win if you don't give up the hope that your wildest dreams are in fact possible. And if you still believe that *someone else* is *better at it* than you (and they may in fact be, right now), then I would challenge you with this: Maybe you have yet to become practiced, disciplined, polished and <u>then</u> discovered. But you have to commit, get better, get moving and ultimately, show up to be considered!

Homework:

You are your greatest teacher about yourself. Fill in the following sentence:

The single thing I do the absolute best, with the least amount of effort is:_____

IDENTITY

The Test

"Trust the test. The test will tell me who I am and where I belong."
-Tris, (Divergent - The movie, 2014)

Knowing who you are is much more important than knowing your purpose. Purpose isn't a one-time event that your life adds up to. It's a never ending string of constant impact that positively advances the lives of other people and it is constantly unfolding and will do so for the rest of your life. It has layers, sensitive time intervals and seasons. It's dependent on your growth, your learning and will open bigger doors of opportunity for you to do higher impact projects that have increasing value and meaning. Knowing who you are will make sure you stay on the correct guided path in the direction of your purpose. It is the wisdom that will keep you on the correct course for your life and allow your dreams to happen faster.

When I was a sophomore in High School (like so many people who were desperate for direction in life) I took one of those career litmus tests which began with a series of weird questions (that is ultimately designed to spit out an answer that will to help you figure out your future, and what the heck to do with your life). For the most part, I already knew the career path I wanted to follow, but decided to take the test anyway, hoping that it would reaffirm what I already knew to be true.

I couldn't wait for the results to arrive! I just knew that it was going to tell me that I was destined to be something cool, like: Comedian, News Reporter or Special Agent, or something crazy and awesome. The litmus test, however, spat out a different answer. It decided that my skills, talents and natural abilities would best be served as: a Funeral Director. This conclusion could not have been farther from the truth!

Sorry to say, but no test on earth can tell you the answer to what you should spend your life doing. Your entire life existence, path and focus cannot be summarized by a standardized test. No machine has the capacity to peak into the future and reveal to you who you are or what you are best at! It's impossible! Everyone is completely unique, and for that reason alone, you are not *built* to fit into a box, rather to be a change agent in the world during the time that you're here. So maximize it! At best, these tests can only point out a few clues. Maybe turn on a few lights in your head. But I will argue that you have your own sensors on the inside of you.

These sensory tools are called your passions, your gut feelings (trust your gut). You know that feeling when something just doesn't feel right or is just not authentically *you.* Conversely, you also know that feeling when something just absolutely gets you excited and causes you to come alive! It's that feeling where you wake up in the morning excited to do that activity. That vigorous feeling that feeds you the energy you need to carry out your task with enthusiasm.

Conversely, just because you're passionate about something, doesn't meant that will turn out to be the thing that you end up making a living out of. But your passions are definitely clues! Follow them. Today I still do voice announcements for radio, TV and on the internet, but those are only a part of my offering to the world, not the entire package. It's not all of who I am but it is definitely part of who I am... ***My highest form of service is: Helping others to realize their hidden potential and get their greatest work into the world (I just so happen to be great at speaking on camera, which helps me in the process.)***

Note: I originally believed that my talent and love for speaking on camera meant that I was supposed to spend my life being a newscaster. I later came to find out that my work would involve not just reaching people through motivational videos, rather traveling the country and helping people with their lives. The talent for the camera was only a <u>tool</u> to help me serve the greater good.

What do you believe to be <u>your</u> highest form of service?

_____

_____

_____

_____

Note: I have the questions, but YOU are the one with the answers. I, nor anyone else can *tell* you who you are, how to be, where you belong, or what part you should be playing in this world. That alone is YOUR choice. My only job is to assist you in the process of getting there.

Note: Be okay with who you are and who you are not.

You are your Strengths:

You might find this hard to believe, but just because you are good at something, it doesn't necessarily mean that *thing* is what you are supposed to be doing for the rest of your life. So often, people are trapped into believing that just because they show the smallest bit of proficiency or talent in one particular area, that it is what they are supposed to major in (in college) or make a career out of. I remember my mom once saying to me: "You know Jarrod, you love cars so much, why don't you try finding a job selling cars?" Except I knew that becoming a car salesman was the last thing I wanted to do. Sometimes people are led to pursuing a career as a professional comedian just because they can make their friends laugh, or into pursuing a medical career just because they like blood and guts, or as a singer just because they can 'hold a few notes'. Don't get me wrong, those are all possibilities, but they may not be the *path*.

Embarrassing story

Growing up, I hated my voice and the way I sounded when I spoke. To this day, I am a voice artist and announcer for commercials but hearing my own recorded voice on audio or video-playback makes me cringe. Go figure. Ironically, everyone else in school loved my voice! Enough to the point where the school staff asked me to deliver the school news and announcements, on-air, both in the morning and afternoon (every day for two-years straight). So I would show up before and after school, study the news scripts and read them live for public broadcast. They made the mistake, however, in figuring that because I possessed a great speaking voice, that I probably also had a great <u>singing</u> voice! Not so! I may speak well but I can barely hold a music note!

So one day, I was approached by a few school members, who were in panic because our high school was hosting a huge local basketball game that night, and the singer who was supposed to sing the live National Anthem, was out sick. Long story made short, they asked me if I would fill in and sing the solo, a cappella (with no accompanying music). I tried my best to convince them that I was not a singer, but no one believed me. So there I was. In the stadium that night. (The announcer): *"Ladies and gentleman. For the singing of our National Anthem, please join me in welcoming, Jarrod Uddin!"* I walked out on the court to the three point line in front of 3-thousand people and all of my peers. I took the microphone. I sang the song. I sounded terrible. It was so bad that I may have given someone cancer! It was the most painful 79-seconds of embarrassment of my human life. Lesson: *Stay in your lane!* End of story.

Note: Don't just go down a path that *seems* right. You want to go down the path that *is* right.

Personally, I am good at:

1. **Cooking:** I love blending together various and complex recipes, and love making food for people. The friends who are closest to me, love to bribe me into cooking and are always willing to drive across town to eat at my house.

2. **Art:** I love sketching, creating oil paintings, drafting and building complex artistic formations for stage plays and large events. Years ago, I was asked to create a custom oil painting of a lady. It took me a few days to finish adding all of the paint layers and details, but what resulted was the most beautiful painting that made her cry when she saw it.

3. **Music:** I have been playing the piano, saxophone and clarinet since before I was 10 years old. I have won music competitions and showcases and love the feeling people get when I play in addition to the audience reaction.

4. **Martial Arts:** I have always loved boxing, learning combat systems, weaponry, and have been training to become a martial arts and kickboxing expert since I was eleven years old. Additionally, I have a passion for physical fitness, swimming and running.

5. **Writing and Public Speaking:** Ever since I was in the first grade, reading and writing have been my favorite subjects. I loved reading aloud in class, participating in Spelling Bees and doing story writing.

Note: This is about finding "what fits".

These are the most identifiable areas that have always been passions and strengths of mine, most of which have been in operation since I could walk and talk. Each of these activities excite me, charge me up and I can't wait to do them. Whether I'm doing item 1, 2, 3, 4, or 5, I usually lose all sense of time while I am doing them, because I love them that much. But not all of them are supposed to be things that I make a full careers out of. Truth be told, it would take a few lifetimes to really do all of them on a grand scale with maximum focus and excellence. Ultimately, I had to decide which one(s) would become vocations, while the others would remain as hobbies and interests.

Today, I am an author, public speaker, motivator and I love investing time, money and focus into bettering myself everyday in these area. So to say the least, Number 5 won out and is the area of passion that receives the most attention, while Martial Arts (Number 4) and Cooking (Number 1) come in second and third place in my focus. From the above list, there is nothing that I love more than speaking, motivating a live audience of people to take action in their lives.

As per my mom's advice about finding a job selling cars, it just so happens that my first job outside of college, was indeed in car sales! I got the chance to travel with the International Auto Show as a Narrator, traveling from city to city, and standing next to a brand new car on a rotating platform, while I got on the microphone and motivated an audience of hundreds of people to buy the model vehicle rotating on stage behind me. My mom expected that I took the job because I loved cars, when in reality it was the opportunity to do public speaking and motivating people that made the job worth my while.

So how do Number 4 and Number 1 fit in? Well, every now and then I am requested and paid to come and substitute teach a martial arts class for various youth sports camps, and every month or so, my friends will try and bribe me into cooking dinner for them. But it is all a pleasure! (And as soon as I have some free time, I plan on purchasing some oil canvases, a set of paints, and a new saxophone in order to serve my other interests).

Begin to pay close attention to *your* interests, passions and the activities that you most enjoy. Every time you find yourself looking forward to an activity, enjoying an activity or feel energized about an activity, write it down. Take note of why you are excited about it. Does this activity allow you to exercise one of your core strengths or passions? What kinds of activities cause the time to fly by when you are doing them?

Note: The world is a much better place when everyone is doing what they do best.

I remember watching a documentary once about the global Pop icon, Beyonce. Several cameras followed her around for a week as the documentary highlighted the performer's work, challenges, and day-to-day activities as she was preparing for one of the most important live performances of her career. With the day-to-day minutia around planning, staging, choreography changes, searching for warehouse spaces to rehearse in, music changes, live rehearsals and other emerging issues, she ended up becoming so consumed with her craft, that she neglected to eat food for a period of over forty-eight hours!

Here is someone that was so focused and passionate about her art that she literally forgot to eat for two whole days! Not eating wasn't something that she intended to do, however, there are times when you can become so focused on your passions and strengths, where you will find that the necessity to eat may just become secondary to your goals. What kinds of activities do you love to do so much that keep you so focused, where the time literally passes you by?

Note: You will always feel excited and energized about certain things such as: hanging out with friends, riding a roller-coaster or just "having fun". You may even feel a strong sense of fulfillment from things like community service or serving in a soup kitchen; activities where your contributions directly impact the life of another individual. You will always get that feeling of fulfillment because our service to others is a requirement for every human being on the planet, and one in which we will always feel sense of purpose. Complete fulfillment in life comes from discovering which passions and talents you should spend the most time on, and then use them to service humanity to your maximum potential.

Conversely, not all strengths are strengths. There are things that you may be great at, that people may even say that you do incredibly well. If, however, these are activities that leave you feeling drained, stressed, unenthused or are things that you don't necessarily look forward to doing, then those are actually called weaknesses!

Strengths: Activities that leave you feeling energized and enthused when doing them. Activities that you look forward to and excel at. Activities that leave you feeling happy and cause the time to go by while doing them. Something you may excel at, or not be very good at, but love doing nonetheless.

Sub-Strengths: These are the activities that you love doing, but don't particularly enjoy investing a great deal of time and energy on. Example: I have strong legs, and I love running and racing people (I always win by the way), however, I used to hate running track in school. This would be a sub-strength, something I excel at and often enjoy, but have discovered (through the time and energy investment) that it is not something that is a passion.

Weaknesses: Activities that you do not look forward to doing. Activities that leave you feeling drained even if it is something that you are good at doing.

Passions: These are the things that you love to do so much, that you would do them for free. Activities that you love learning about, talking about and spending time on. Activities that you find yourself practicing over and over and getting better at each time. Things that make the time fly. My advice is to learn to do your passions well enough that someone is willing to pay you for it.

Note: People love to hire and work with people who are passionate about what they do.

The Passion Test:

All of my life I have loved running outdoors and racing people for fun, so my parents thought it would be a great idea for me to join the track team in high school. I absolutely hated it. With all of the conditioning, running "ladders" (training) I had to discover that running was an activity that I enjoyed for fun, but not for serious competition. This is an example of something that was a strength, interest, a bit of a passion even, but it would only become a weakness the more I would have to invest into it.

So here's the test: Once you have identified your top five or ten strengths, passions and activities that you love, begin to do some research. Read about them, study the pros, seek practice and add to your mastery in those areas. Join some sort of extracurricular or civic groups where you can exercise those strengths. You will soon begin to discover which ones you really love and want to invest further in, and conversely, which ones you really don't want to spend that much time on. Your real passions are those items that you find yourself not being able to live without doing. The stuff that you don't mind sacrificing for, pouring time and resources into in order to keep them alive and going.

Note: Passions that we never knew that we had can also come to the surface when we are in a place where we can develop our greatest strengths. Do you know what yours are?

Another Note: Ignore your passions, and you will be robbing yourself of the best chance at happiness that you will ever have!

DON'T LOOK TO PERFECT YOUR WEAKNESSES

Sometimes you can end up doing a thing for so long that you end up becoming great at it, but if at the end of the day it doesn't energize you or bring you an honest sense of joy and fulfillment, it will still leave you feeling drained. For example: Almost every member in my family are close to expert golfers. There is almost nothing they love more than heading out to their favorite golf course and playing eighteen holes. My grandparent's golf, both my mother and father golf several times per week and win golf tournaments every year. Even my Godparents are LPGA instructors! Their time "out on the links" is their relaxation, their love and time spent that leaves them feeling rejuvenated and whole. I call them "the masters" of the game.

My dad started me out by putting a golf club in my hands as a toddler and had me out on the golf course "swinging away" as a small kid on Saturday mornings. I took up the game as an interest because everyone in my family loved the activity, so I figured it would do me some good to give it a shot. I have now been playing the game for so long (and have received so much training from "the masters") that I have become quite the proficient. But no matter how hard I tried, I could never quite <u>enjoy</u> the game like they did.

Are there activities that you have been focusing on, working on, or perfecting that are still leaving you feeling drained at the end of the day? Have you been working more on your weaknesses as opposed to building on your strengths and passions? I must say this as a little disclaimer: Having some proficiency in your areas of weakness is not a bad thing. It can sometimes pay off nicely! I once took a golf course in college as an elective and (an "easy A+"). I was the only one in the class with training and talent in that area. As a result, not only did I receive outstanding scores, but I was able to help other students in the class who were struggling and even made a few friends in the process. A few of whom are close friends to this day.

Additionally, although music was another of my sub-strengths, it was my training as a musician that helped me to win me a two-year scholarship into the college of my choice. Although I haven't picked up a musical instrument since, it can very well be your sub-strengths or even weaknesses that ultimately open the doors of opportunity.

Some BAD advice:

"It's bad advice to tell people to follow their passions...." -
Anonymous Contributor

This was the title of a recent online article which hundreds of people chimed in with their opinion via social media. As a person who believes in following one's passions, I of course had to fire back with a strong argument that caused pandemonium, tons of "likes" and the article writer *"following-me-back"* in the end (I'm not bragging... I'm just saying). Initially the writer had argued that there is no such thing as pre-existing passion, and that we should all: *just pick something, perfect it, and get so good at it, that you get noticed by someone who can hire and pay you.* In other words, pick a weakness. Any weakness. Get really good at it. Build an entire life around it and you'll be successful. That recommendation is actually the "bad advice". That is the easiest way to lead a miserable life and become a future quitter!

But let's play devil's advocate for a second. Let's suppose you do follow this advice, by just picking a weakness, and master it to the extent of making a career out of it. Let's now play this scenario out to its conclusion. You may just end up getting a great job with great benefits that allows you to provide a good life for yourself and your family. But here's the problem. You won't be truly happy. You won't be passionate about what you do. You will end up going to work every day, not because you enjoy it. Not because you want to. But because you have to! You will dread every morning when the alarm clock goes off and will feel drained at the end of the day, because you have officially made a living out of a weakness.

These are the people who have the proverbial quarter-life and midlife crisis, and panic over the questions: *What am I really doing here? Where in the world is my life headed?* These are the people who may have temporary moments of enjoyment in their lives but don't have true fulfillment. They are the ones who end up hating their lives in 20-years. All they want to do is escape the misery, but now they have added on to their lives: a spouse, kids, a mortgage, two cars, daycare and several other bills to pay, and now feel like they are so rooted in their patterns that it's too late to back out of it or do anything else. At night they lay in bed, in silence, and agonize over the looming thought: *What IF I would've been courageous enough to try that business idea or follow the path of my <u>real</u> passion, or had been brave enough to take the chance to do what I <u>really</u> wanted to do.* They feel stuck.

When you feel stuck, you are not passionate. People who lack passion are not "extra-milers". These are the ones who show up to work and only meet the bare minimum requirements. They do just enough to not get fired but feel exhausted by the end of the day. They are the ones who try and create their life purpose around a spouse, kids, or a shiny new car, or a host of other *things* that they believe will make them happy, but it never lasts long. Real happiness and true fulfillment comes from mastering your strengths and passions first. Mastering a weakness may allow you to survive and do a few things in life, but the best that it will ever allow you to be, is *average*. That's just downright depressing, and is definitely no way to live your life.

Note: It's far easier and certainly more enjoyable to master your strengths than your weaknesses.

Another Note: Do not be the *What IF* person.

So what are *your* strengths?

My STRENGTHS:

Strength:

_____

_____

_____

_____

What about this activity do you love?

_____

_____

_____

_____

What about this activity gives you strength?

_____

_____

_____

_____

My WEAKNESSES:

Weakness:

_____

_____

_____

_____

What about this activity do you dislike?

_____

_____

_____

_____

What about this activity drains you?

_____

_____

_____

_____

Once you identify what your top strengths and passions are, the next logical step is to develop them by finding "scenes", places and activities where you can put these strengths and passions to work.

Possible places (scenes) where I can exercise my strengths:

Location 1: *Example. Radio station where I am an intern....*

How I see myself contributing at this location:

_____

_____

_____

_____

Location 2: *Example. Morning announcements at school...*

How I see myself contributing at this location:

_____

_____

_____

_____

Location 3: *Example. Soup kitchen (I'm great at cooking and being kind to people)*

How I see myself contributing at this location:

_____

_____

_____

_____

Location 4:

How I see myself contributing at this location:

_____

_____

_____

_____

Figuring it all out

You may still be wondering: '*How can I serve the world with my strengths? And learn how to do it well enough that someone is willing to pay me for it*'? This is what I believe: At least one life changing opportunity comes along for each of us every single day. Our senses are just untrained to recognize it when it appears. It always starts out as something that you feel strongly that you need to do or should do. Conversely, the same feeling will occur when you know you really should *not* be doing something. Honor that gut feeling. Sometimes that brilliant opportunity is disguised as *work* or a task that no one else wants to do. The key to being rewarded for your strengths is to focus by building on it, adding to it and doing as much as you can to become even stronger in that area. Don't just settle for *good*. Go for *mastery* level. The more you focus on that strength the more opportunities you will begin to notice that have always been there.

Note: People will celebrate someone who gives a good effort... But they will idolize someone who displays mastery!

Note: Many times we are pushed into doing something, or pursuing something only because someone else needs us to fill a particular role at a particular time. You may have some talent in a particular area, but it doesn't necessarily mean you need to go out and do that thing as a career. Other times you may start off doing something that is not the *thing*, but it could end up leading to the *thing* you feel you were always meant to do.

Like me, you probably also have talent in several areas. It is very unlikely, however, that we will find the time or capacity to make a lucrative and focused career out of ALL of those areas of interest. That would be a bit unrealistic, even though people have told me that I need to open a restaurant because they love my cooking or that I should open up a martial arts school because I'm great at teaching kids martial arts at summer camps or that I should go be a radio host. That's nice, but what I've learned is that some things will be vocation, while others will just be hobbies and interests that others will enjoy from me.

<u>Homework:</u> *Your "Passion" Project*

I want you to spend some time this week working on one of your strengths, passions or something that you love to be involved in that ultimately brings you fulfillment. For me, my passion project was doing the morning announcements broadcast over the P.A system at my school every morning for two-years. The role allowed me to utilize my greatest strengths, passions and made me excited to wake up early every single morning excited to perform the task. What is yours?

It could be a morning workout that helps you condition for a sports team, reading, and working on a large group project, practicing music or community service. As long as it is an activity that brings you a feeling of energy, fulfillment and inspires you to get out-of-bed in the morning and moving, then go for it. (If no activity comes to mind then go back a few pages and start off with the strengths exercises).

WHEN YOUR DAY JOB DOESN'T GIVE YOU MEANING

Serving at the pleasure of your 9-5.

The Nine to Five. It's your most common source of income but oftentimes a common source of discontent and unhappiness. If you're like most people, you've been in school all of your life and possibly couldn't wait to just start working somewhere post graduation. The chance to finally earn some money, have some independence and realize the value of your education and potential. But if not planned carefully, your nine to five day job could go from being a much awaited opportunity to a pain point that never gives you the satisfaction that you crave.

Other times, people are content on their jobs until their bosses want them to spend time strengthening their weak points and improve in the areas where they may be lacking. Having to work on areas that we dread thinking about can be a total fear factor for most people. One thing to sober up on is when it comes to happiness, it is not the job of our employers to make us content or fulfilled. Their job is to align us with the purpose and vision of the company and make sure that we are operating at peak capacity and potential, whether we are happy or not. Our job is to show up with a great attitude while remaining teachable, trainable and coachable.

The common misconception of one's current day job is thinking that it's the totality of your career. It's not. And it can quickly change. The other misconception is that there aren't many other options available. But there are.

Knowing yourself, who you are and who you are not, is one of the most powerful virtues that you can arm yourself with when seeking fulfillment. I've known people who are into their professions, making a ton of money, driving their dream cars and to the world it looks like they have it all. But come to find out, they are still unfulfilled. For some, they feel their work is mundane, boring, and they aren't making any difference or having any impact. They feel their efforts are overlooked, and that there must be more to life than what they are currently doing, even though they are making a lot of money.

At some point, we all often come to these points where we may find ourselves unfulfilled with our current circumstances, location, home, money and wonder what's next? Or if better is even available. I remember my first job out of college was as a youth motivational speaker. I was living a rockstar life, being paid by companies to travel all around the country and motivate audiences. But there weren't any raises available, no advancement or mentorship offered, and after two years, I felt like I hit a glass ceiling. I wanted more. More money. More meaning and impact. I just didn't know how to get there.

It was around this time when one of my mentors taught me a simple, yet valuable lesson about both knowing myself and a strategy that would help me uncover where i should go next on my life journey, especially when we are seeking meaning and purpose. Step one is just admitting that you are unsatisfied while looking inward to really pinpoint what it is that you are unhappy about. Maybe the core of your dissatisfaction involves a task that drains you. Maybe it's you're lacking a good manager or leadership that has no interest in coaching you to your greater potential (or is inept to do so). Maybe you're working a job that you only took in order to pay the bills, but it is not fulfilling you in any way. Maybe you're content but deep down you just want more.

When this happens, you're in perfect position to learn an incredible deal about yourself! Usually this is the lesson that dissatisfaction teaches us. Start by grabbing 5 new file folders and begin to label each of them according to the top 5-10 things you are passionate about. They can be labeled with titles like: Travel, Design, Reading, Products, Health, just as an example. Whatever your core passions, interests and hobbies are, they should each have their own folder. Step two of the process is embarking on a journey called 'hunt and gather'. Begin collecting magazine articles, tear sheets, photos, information and anything exciting that you can find surrounding your core passions and interests and add them into each of the designated file folders.

Personally, I've always known that speaking, writing and motivating others were my chief passions (in addition to travel, cooking and high octane activities: roller coaster rides, skydiving and thrills). I began to gather articles on subjects that I really wanted to learn about, information that inspired me that I would ultimately enjoy teaching other people. Any quotes, books, motivational videos or photos that pertained to achievement and inspiring people, I gathered and relocated to one folder (in addition to cool food recipes and travel ideas to locations that boasted high octane activities each went in their separate folders).

When you do this consistently, you will notice that opportunities begin to arise that allow for expression of these interests or even ways to incorporate some of these passions into your daily work. When you do these activities and focus on gathering items for your folders, you will simultaneously be training your mind to look for opportunities to live out those pictures and interests that you have been gathering (life imitates art). But surprisingly, each of these areas are connected in some form or fashion. All of these key interests make up the real 'you' and will be a part of your future while some end up being a part of your vocation and others as hobbies.

The more information you add to your folders, answers will start to develop and unfold in those key areas, but only when you take action! Action is the chief ingredient to making all of this happen. About a week into this 'hunt and gather' I stumbled across an inspirational article on another author and speaker who was doing the kind of work that I had dreamed of doing. He was also living the kind of life that I wanted to live (on his own terms), making a ton of money in the process. I decided to follow him on social media and then learned about an upcoming opportunity to meet him in person and learn his time tested strategies that would help me to have the same kind of success. Today, I am a full time speaker and author, while my other filed categories of interests are activities that I enjoy in my spare time as a recharge.

This process is all about Self-awareness. Every one of us owes it to ourselves to really get acquainted with ourselves again! Unfulfillment is the warning sign that you have not been honoring your first love. This is how you learn about yourself, where you might fit and what to do next when where you are at isn't satisfactory. This process helps you understand what you're good at and what you suck at. This is where you learn that the career you thought you'd want might not be the one for you and that it might be time to jump ship.

Knowing who you are is paramount to your identity. To know who you are you must be able to clearly identify your strengths and weaknesses and be able to articulate it well. I like to think of it like this: You are your strengths. You are not your weaknesses. But knowing both helps you identify who you are and who you are not. And when you are armed with this information, no one can drive your life off course without your permission.

Knowing who you are.

Knowing who you are is much more important than knowing your purpose. Purpose isn't a one-time event that your life adds up to. It's a never ending string of constant impact that positively advances the lives of other people and it is constantly unfolding and will do so for the rest of your life. It has layers, sensitive time intervals and seasons. It's dependent on your growth, your learning and will open bigger doors of opportunity for you to do higher impact projects that have increasing value and meaning. Knowing *who* you are will make sure you stay on the correct guided path in the direction of your purpose. It is the wisdom that will keep you on the correct course for your life and allow your dreams to happen faster.

Ever had a job that you *hated?*

One of the first part-time jobs I ever had in school was at a dental laboratory as a cleaning specialist. My job was to file down crowns for people's teeth and perform the brutally menial task of plucking small rubber pieces from rubber pads. It was miserable work that left your fingertips feeling sore and useless at the end of the day. I learned that something kind of awesome happens when you *feel stuck* doing an activity or job that you hate. Your brain begins to imagine where it is that you would really rather be. In those moments it hit me that I would really rather be mentoring young adults rather than blasting crowns all day.

Sometimes, that is how it happens. So if you are undecided about what your strengths or passions are, don't be afraid to just take a leap and get started somewhere, doing something, and finding what fits. Once there, don't quit on the first week. Stay long enough to complete a project or task. Give yourself some time before you quit.

Find something that you love about it, master it, look for the little glimpses of impact that the role is allowing you to have in the bottom-line of the business, the clients or customers you service (even if it is nothing more than a friendly smile that you provide on the front line – that can have the power to brighten someone's day). Find it and specialize in it. Something amazing begins to happen (we end up moving from move from line-workers, capable of doing a process over and over, to being artists that are capable of blending what we feel deeply compelled to be, do, or say into our daily tasks, routines or jobs). Find your *thing* in the process that can maybe be tweaked, made better, even if it is just a better way to deliver a welcome, humanize or simplify a process, and insert your twist.

Note: Just get started

WE ALL
NEED A SIDE
HUSTLE

We love opportunity. But opportunity doesn't always love us or provide us with the satisfaction that we crave. Personally, there have been jobs that I have given my heart and soul to, that have had to let me go, due to the business shutting down. So while your first job out of school may have been a great opportunity initially, you may still be craving more. More opportunity to flourish, grow and become more of the person that you already are and do more of what you love.

So maybe it's time for a side hustle. This is where you pursuit other areas of interest that may not always pay you extra money, but maybe it's volunteer work, an apprenticeship or a project that adds to your skill base, teaches you something new or grants you some valuable career experience and unlock some hidden talents. Oftentimes these side hustles can open the doors to a whole new job or career field that is way more fulfilling than your current role. And at the very least, it can be a temporary means of escape and relief from where you are currently.

Maybe you've always dreamed of building websites and you decide to take some free coding classes twice a week at a trade school. Maybe you've always dreamed of being a photographer so you decide to assist a professional photographer and gain some valuable industry insights before you decide to make the career switch. Maybe you decide to spearhead a community event project for a pro bono service organization that you joined. These side hustles can earn you extra money, unveil new talents, and even exercise a level of creativity that your current position does not allow.

Even when I was employed in my first dream job outside of college, I had several side hustles. I started up a side business with a network marketing company where I got to learn the thrilling art of sales, along with building and training a team from scratch. On the weekends I volunteered with show production company and worked a sound board to provide audio support for live concerts. That same production company recruited me to join their acting troop that produced a string of motivational independent films that are viewed around the world. Each of these opportunities has garnered me new groups of friends, invaluable experiences, has helped me make a difference in my community, and has stacked my resume with value add projects that my one day job could never have supplied me with.

The point is, even if you have your dream job, own your own business, or are employed in the area of your greatest strength, we all still need a side hustle. There are areas of potential and interests that one job or business cannot possibly accommodate. The side hustle guarantees that we keep on learning, growing, continue meeting new people and making an impact abroad and in the community around us. Find your next side hustle.

IMITATION IS SUICIDE

"Being your authentic self is the most important formula for success that there is" - Life & Success Coach Dr. Stacia Pierce

Comparison is unwise:

"Jarrod… why can't you be more like Chris..???", said my mom. I grew up with Chris. He was always taller than me, more athletic, a big hit with all of the girls at our school, hung out with all the cool kids and was certainly more popular than I was. As you can imagine, I was the opposite. I was not tall. I had zero "swagger". I was rhythmically challenged (for a Black-guy). I had a head shaped like a bean with a bald spot. All things that made me self-conscious and lacking in confidence. Not to mention getting picked on by bigger kids. Chris and I weren't exactly friends, but it just so happens that our moms were close friends, hence the connection.

I remember this being one of the most angry and embarrassing experiences of my life. I was 12 going on 13, and as if I wasn't already having the prepubescent identity crisis that comes along with being 12, the one thing I did not want is to be compared to someone else (as if how I was *showing-up* in the world was less than good enough). My mom could just as easily have said: '*You know, I really don't like you all that much… You really weren't the child that I expected to have*'. The rest of what she had to say regarding my image, was no 'walk in the park', and as if the shame and embarrassment of not feeling accepted by the one person who I thought was supposed to like me for who I was and how I was, the truth is - I didn't like myself all that much either.

Note: For me, that is where the unhealthy need for "approval" began.

I didn't know much about who I was or what I was supposed to be doing in the world. I resented the fact that I wasn't as tall as other people, super athletic or display any superhuman talents or proclivities. The girls that I did like, didn't like me back. I didn't have that much swagger... all combinations that didn't make me so popular at that age. But the one thing that I did know is that I didn't want to be compared to someone else who I didn't think I could be anyway. The struggle for acceptance left me feeling empty and I needed to fill that void with *something*. Like many people struggling to deal with life, food ultimately became my drug of choice to cope with not feeling 'good enough', which led to me gaining almost 30-pounds in one school year, further adding to my low self-esteem.

Note: At that young age, when craving approval and acceptance, humanity often distracts us with this little idea: *If you're not getting the results you want, then find someone else who is and just copy them.*

"Being yourself may actually be easier than the illusion that imitation is better" - Uncle Mel

The problem is that I wasn't very good at *copying* or imitating others. I did manage to later make a few cool-kids friends, but the problem was in order to keep those friends one would have to do what they did to remain accepted. Things that I was not accustomed to doing: (Stealing, lying, skipping class, doing drugs, etc.). I remember we would sneak out of school at lunch time and go to a place across the street that had really good food. Sometimes my friends would pay for their items but mostly they got their thrills from stealing, and of course they would try to get me to be involved. Because I had created these so-called friendships out of the sheer desire for acceptance I felt like I couldn't turn away from the things they wanted me to do with them, for the fear of losing what associations I had managed to build.

Ultimately it hit me, the unavoidable reality: These were not *real* friendships. I thought to myself, *'what am I doing? This isn't like me, this isn't how I was raised to be or act'.* I finally accepted the truth of what I had been trying to avoid: I was paying the ultimate price by giving other people the power to decide for me who I would be and how I would be, all for the reward of temporary *acceptance.*

Comparison Is Suicide

Late one evening, while spending the night at my grandparents' house, I happened to find one of my grandfather's' hand guns on the top shelf in the coat closet. It was wintertime in Michigan and I had left my hat and gloves laying out. Being late at night, my grandmother had retired for the evening to her bedroom, and being a bit of a *neat freak,* I knew she wouldn't be pleased to find my stuff laying on the sofa the next morning. So I grabbed my gloves, reached way up above my head to the top shelf of the coat closet and pushed some other items aside to locate space to put away my things. As I did so, my hand swept across the pistol. I immediately knew what the item was as soon as I felt it. Recalling my elementary classroom training regarding the danger of guns, contrasted with the sudden reality that I was actually touching one, made me freeze where I stood.

My grandfather, at that time was an active police officer in the city of Detroit, and had plenty of weapons stashed around the house in special hiding places. At twelve years old, and still pretty short, I reached back up, grabbed the gun and pulled it down. It was late at night. The house was quiet, dark, and calm. Everything was still, except for a faint sound coming from the TV in the den down the hall, where my grandfather was napping. There's something chilling about silence and calm that forces you to *face yourself,* your issues, the things you've been avoiding and the things you fear most. Right then and all at once, my issues, insecurities, realities, pain and shame came rushing to the surface. I wasn't who I wanted to be and had nearly given up on the hope of ever being *good enough.*

It was the first time I had ever held a loaded weapon. The metal on the gun was so cold and heavy, as was the prospect of going through with what came next in my mind. As I stood there in the hallway staring into a gaze, I had finally concluded to ask myself the inevitable question, which so many depressed people wrestle with internally: *Am I better off dead?* I stood there for what felt like hours, pondering.

So much went through my mind in those moments. Wondering at what point my grandfather would wake up and catch me standing there in the hallway, with his weapon in hand, I began to fear for how much trouble I would be in. Nonetheless, something inside of me screamed: *'Just do it!' Hurry up! Get it over with'.* Then I started thinking: Would it be messy? Would it be loud? More than the prospect of taking my own life, I think I was more afraid of making a mess on the floor that my grandmother had cleaned only hours prior.

All of a sudden, in that moment... I *committed*. I had made up in my mind that I was going to *do it.* And right then at the point of execution, I discovered that something interesting happens when you decide to *commit.* Just when I fell into believing that my life was miserable and that no one cared about me, all of a sudden, everyone that really did care about me, came to mind; Every person that ever made a positive impact or deposit into my life was right there on the front lines of my heart and conscience, starting with my grandfather. We had a good day that day. One of his favorite pastimes was driving me around the city for what seemed like hours of deep conversation.

He would talk to me the entire time, sharing with me every life lesson he could think to teach. I was his first and only grandson and a primary investment. My baby sister, who was recently born in that same year, came next in my mind. Amazingly, she never cried when I held her. To her it didn't matter if I was imperfect. My presence alone was all she needed. My parents nicknamed me her "security blanket". Everyone who cared for me, from my mom, to my extended family and neighbors even, all rushed through my mind. In that moment I realized that the number of those who loved and accepted me far outweighed those who did not.

Who was I to give up on life because a few people at school wouldn't accept me for who I was? I imagined for a moment that I had actually gone through with it, pulling the trigger, and then later coming back to explain to my grieving family and friends, *why* I did it. Every reason that I could come up with sounded like crap, selfish and a pile of weak excuses. I put the gun back, and for the first time, I felt *relief*.

I made up my mind that I was tired of conforming to "fit in". Right then, I decided that I was going to stand up for myself, for what I knew was right and without caring how many so-called friends I would lose in the process. Peace came over me. When I returned to school the following week, I amazingly had no problems. I simply refused to do things that were outside of my character. Saying "no" was easy. There's something about having an internal resolve that others come to respect. I learned that people are far more likely to accept someone who is strong enough to stand up for what they believe in rather than follow blindly. I ended up not losing friends. Instead, many of them began to adjust to my standards. The few who wouldn't, eventually removed themselves from the picture, which ultimately made *room* for new friends to come in.

Note: To be at peace is the best reward available.

Here's the thing…

It may seem easier at times to just follow people's expectations of you in order to avoid friction and "ruffled feathers", but the price will always be much greater. It is much harder, however, to be *who* you know you should be, while staring in the very face of adversity, to stand up for yourself when it's not popular, and all while not worrying about what other people think. This option is more rewarding. No matter how many people disagree with you, refuse to accept you, or how many friends you may lose. It's okay. Let them go their separate ways. If you lose some *approval* ratings in the process for not being whom *others* want you to be, then they weren't your real friends to begin with.

Note: Again, let them go! New and better friends will come along!

The "*Approval*" Addiction

Despite having struggled with feeling "good enough" in the eyes of my parents, they were still loving and moral people, who believed in honesty and in doing the right thing. I had always been raised to show respect, work hard, and all of the things that make someone a "good" person. Stealing, lying, and avoiding responsibility was definitely not a part of the formula. And every time I had felt pressure to do it without taking a stand against it, I felt horrible; Like I was denying my own identity; Like a piece of me was suffering as I was tried to fit in and be accepted by others' low standards. The **Approval Addiction,** as I call it, wasn't worth it.

The Approval Addiction (defined): Seeking the approval of others to give you a sense of self-worth instead of generating it internally. This is basically when you do things simply to get others to like or accept you. The problem with this is that these individuals that you are looking to please, only put up with you because you are basing your identity on who they think you should be or who they want you to be for the moment. The other problem with this is it doesn't speak to your authentic nature. You will find yourself having to constantly compromise your morals, values and pay *their* price of admission, while slowly denying yourself. And as soon as *they* decide that they are done with you, you will be replaced or thrown away. How depressing is that!?

People only have an **approval addiction** when they don't know who they are, so they must constantly depend on other people to approve or like them. Ultimately, when you take a bold stand for who you are and what you believe, people may not agree or like it, but they will have to respect you for boldly standing up for yourself. Truthfully here's the **secret:** They too struggle with their identity. They are only acting like that because they don't know who they are either. So they deal with it by doing dumb-stuff for the thrill of it, as an attempt to alleviate their own internal *pain.*

A little basic psychology: Truthfully, *they* would love to be able to stand up for themselves and be strong, feel loved, confident, powerful, respected, and secure within themselves, but they won't because they don't know how, or where to start. Their misery still needs 'company', a 'sidekick', and that is where I came in, until I decided that *enough was enough*. There were times where seeing me develop my own identity and strength, roused the envy within them. Oftentimes, people will dislike you simply because you have found the courage to do something or become the *somebody* that you've always wanted, something that they wish they could do. That bit of strength within *you* often pokes at *their* inner weakness, leaving them feeling like they only have one of two options: Either change and get better or despise the person who displays the strength that *they* wish they had. Instead of attacking *you* the smart thing to do would be to attack their own insecurities.

Note: People who have decided to 'unfollow the crowd' are not concerned with people's objections to them being their authentic selves, nor do they ponder much over the thought: *'But what if they don't like me for it?'* (If I were you I would care less).

The longer you study someone else, you will slowly begin to make excuses for why you can't achieve something, try harder or win in life. It is one thing to have someone as a guidepost, mentor or someone you look up to that sharpens you, motivates you, and helps you to improve your overall performance. It is, however, quite another thing to reject your own authenticity while chasing after someone else's.

It's the sheer thinking that someone else only has what they have because of how they (look, walk, talk, act, who they know or how they dress), rather than the effort that they give; an effort that you in fact have not. The longer you focus on them, the more you recognize how different you are in contrast. Eventually you will develop a distaste for yourself for not being like (them) or having what they have. Ultimately, instead of celebrating and building on your own uniqueness, you in turn (beat yourself up) and despise yourself for it. You have now effectively fooled yourself into thinking that you will never be worthy of good things in life because you are not *like* (*him or her*) all while comparing and judging.

This is the very deception in making comparisons of yourself to other people. It causes **depression**, which I define as: *The inability to construct and visualize a good and happy future for one's self*, which is impossible if you are focused on someone else in comparison to who you are *not*, thereby disqualifying yourself from achievement. Failure to discontinue the unhealthy comparisons will only increase your risks for depression, which leads to suffering, potential substance abuse and suicidal thoughts. In my book, *comparison is suicide*. Stop it!

You are needed!

The entire world is waiting to see who you are going to *be,* but nobody wants to see you be a duplicate. There are already plenty of societal expectations, pressures and messages out there about who to be and how to be, but who will you *choose* to be? Have you ever thought about why you were not born one-hundred years ago? Or five-hundred years ago? In my glorious opinion, I would argue that you weren't born back then because you weren't *needed* back then, but you are here today because you are needed for today.

True Story

A good friend of mine, Robin, once told me of the abusive relationship between her mother and father. Robin's mother was already months pregnant with her, but her father wanted the pregnancy terminated through an abortion, which would eliminate Robin's chances of ever being born. When her mother refused to have an abortion, her father at one point pushed her to the ground and commenced to punching her in the stomach. Robin is unsure how long the abuse lasted, but feels blessed to have been born without medical complications, and to be alive and well to this day. She went on in life to do great things, winning academic and music awards while we were in high school, a full-college scholarship, and even created a unique education program that has revolutionized the speed at which thousands of children learn to read, write and retain information so that they can have an advantage in life. No matter how hard her own father fought to keep her from being born, she made it, and was indeed needed for today, and so are <u>you</u>.

The Greatest Battle You will ever fight...

Consider this: During <u>conception</u> *you* were the *one* sperm that made it to the egg! That means that you fought your way past one-hundred million others for first place, and won! That tells me, that your getting here was the most serious battle you've ever endured and that you are supposed to be here. No matter what circumstances that you came here under, please accept the fact that *however* you arrived, you and your authentic self, fought to be here. You've earned your right to live because you fought for it.

"...and if you can just do <u>you</u>, well enough, you'll be phenomenal" - *Josh Shipp*

Homework:

The approval addiction, or the need to be accepted and validated, is rooted in low self-esteem. A self-love deficit. The more you love and appreciate yourself and the things that make you unique, the more others will be curious to learn about you as well. I want you to begin thinking about some of the things that make you unique, special, and different from others. Write them down here:

_____

_____

_____

_____

Lastly, I want you to use the rest of this page to write out 30-things that you LOVE about yourself. This is a challenging one. Not everyone can get up to number 30. Even if you have to pause, take a few days and then come back to it, that's fine. We are still in the self-discovery phase. The point is, the more we pay attention to, appreciate and invest in the things that make us different, special or unique, the greater our self-esteem. The greater our self-esteem, the happier we become.

30 - Things I love about myself:

KNOW YOUR *ACHILLES* HEEL

In Greek mythology, Achilles was a baby facing a premature death sentence. To prevent an early death, his mother took him to a river that was told to offer mystical powers of invulnerability. As she dipped baby Achilles in the water he was endowed with invulnerability, however, the one part of his body that was untouched by the water, was his heel, the very part of his body that his mother held him by as she dipped him in the water. Achilles grew into a powerful warrior over the years and survived many battles, until he was shot in the ankle by a poisoned arrow, leading to his demise. It was quite literally, Achilles' heel, his only weakness that led to his death.

In my book, your "Achilles Heel" is the weakness that also hurts you and harms your potential. These are the weaknesses that are serious and require your immediate attention. The key is refusing to protect or hide them, but to own, face and fix them before they become your very downfall.

True story

One of my best friends, Sam, who recently graduated college, is one of the most talented people I know in the realm of computer programming. Give him a computer and he can make it do almost anything. He can build or fix any website, troubleshoot complex algorithms and create almost any application you can think of. Even more important, he loves doing it. This is his greatest strength and a skill that is highly in demand to any employer.

But his 'Achilles Heel' is in the realm of his communication. His texts, emails and comments usually come across as offensive, although unintentionally. He virtually has no 'filter' and tends to say whatever is on his mind, good or bad. It tends to get him in trouble. He is a business owner as well. And when you are in business, you need for people to like you as well as buy from you. People want to do business with people they like, not just people who are passionate about what they do. Sam's communication is more than a weakness. It's his 'Achilles Heel'. We all have that one weakness that we need to work on, because without doing so, we choose to hold ourselves back from achieving our maximum potential in life.

Note: People who have decided to 'unfollow the crowd' are aware of the things that trip them up and inhibit their success. They face it and they DEAL with it, no matter how painful the process may be. Here are your options when you have identified your 'Achilles Heel':

Option 1: Bury or ignore it

Option 2: Own it

Option 3: Own it and commit to doing something about it

Story continued…

Sam finally gave in, understanding that if he didn't work on his 'Achilles Heel', that it might cause him to lose out on some great opportunities in his near future. We began to practice every single day, working on interview questions and responses. Even the kinds of hand gestures and non-verbal's that the interviewers would consider pleasant or offensive. For him, facing his greatest weakness was quite uncomfortable, painful and I could sense him getting weary and frustrated with the process. But he did not quit. He understood that the career, money and lifestyle that he wanted, was right on the other side of conquering this weakness, or at least enough to ace the interview.

He ended up being invited to interview for several companies. Some companies liked him so much that they invited him for a second, third and some a fourth round of interviews, flying him out to their headquarters on all-expenses paid trips! Eventually he got hired for a paid internship with one of the top social media companies in the world that paid him a huge salary for the summer months, provided free housing, a maid, free food and a number of enviable perks. Once he graduated college, he got recruited for an even better job and is living his dream life, doing what he loves the most - all because he was willing to work on the one thing that was inhibiting his success, his "Achilles Heel".

Note: When we have spent a great deal of time wrestling with a weakness that has become an 'Achilles Heel', we become accustomed to it, build our lives around it and tend to protect it from change. Similar to how individuals with health issues will often put up a fight when it comes to visiting the doctor, we humans, will protect the things that we are afraid to change (for fear of inconvenience). Sometimes the drug of choice feeds the issue that we are masking, and anyone that comes along to inquire about the issue, we will fight. It is in our nature (similar to the way an animal with a wounded leg will fiercely protect it by lashing at you before it allows you to help them to fix it.

Who are you going to be when the "walls come down"?

Ancient history tells us the story of a city named Jericho, one of the most beautiful, fruitful and coldest cities in the world, that was once captured and overrun by a small group of soldiers.

In those days, ancient rulers would have massive walls built around their entire city for the purpose of protection from outside military forces. The size of a city's wall represented their power and military strength. A clear warning to all who would dare attempt a challenge. Hence, the higher the wall, the greater the city. Jericho's wall was indeed massive.

One day, preluding a great battle, Jericho's massive wall of protection was crumbled, and taken down by a small, rag-tag group of soldiers who sought to regain possession of the ancient city that originally belonged to them. The inhabitants therein engaged in a fearsome battle with the small opposing army, but were soon defeated, destroyed and lost their city.

The point of this story: In life, we all have *things* that we deal with. Issues that we choose to protect rather than resolve, confront or fix. They are usually things in our humanity - mistakes, weaknesses and embarrassing things that we fear others will discover about us, possibly use against us or just the sheer thought of being exposed for the weaknesses we're choosing to hide. Our most feeble attempts to *cover up* are usually achieved by "putting up walls" around the very issues that we want hidden and protected from passersby, trying our very best to act as if the issue we're hiding doesn't exist.

How do you *act* or respond when your wall is *under attack*? What is your wall? For some people, their wall might be: *Lying, putting on a fake smile, making excuses, turning angry and aggressive, willing to become enraged and fist fight if necessary*. These just a few of the many "walls" we erect in our lives. They are expensive, high maintenance and all for the sake of protecting a weakness.

Please understand that no "wall" is completely impenetrable. Something as tiny as a hairline crack in the foundation, can cause even the strongest of walls to collapse, exposing the secrets hidden within. I will argue that the energy, intensity and exhaustion it takes to construct a wall, maintain the wall and fight, is not worth it. Are you willing to own, confront and deal with your weaknesses? Because if not, the wall will sooner or later come crashing down, exposing you for everything you've been hiding. Who will you become when that happens?

Question to consider: What weaknesses do you have, that you overcompensate for, that others don't know you have? What is that *thing* you're protecting from change?

What is YOURS?

_____

_____

_____

What does protecting it do for you?

_____

_____

_____

Are you willing to do something about it?

YES ___

NO ___

What one thing can you do about it today? Just one small step…

_____

_____

_____

Note: The best thing we can do to *fear* is confront it.

"A Painful Fall From Glory"

We have all heard about, read about and witnessed the rise and fall of several of our nation's top young celebrity artists. Even with all of their talent, good looks, fame and fortune, they too have weaknesses just like everyone else. Oftentimes we are fooled into believing that fame and fortune has the power to "fix" and make us better. The lie's we are fooled into believing, that if we can manage to acquire fame and fortune, that our lives would be easier.

Because our culture funnels so much love and admiration towards our celebrities, their images and talents, we often allow them to enter the world's spotlight and rise to glorified statuses without requiring them to first "grow up". By default, they remain emotionally stagnant and immature with larger than life bank accounts.

When we as a community allow this to happen, we end up making them victims of their talent, and later punishing them when they stumble, make a mistake or fall short of being a *positive role model*. The very fortune they managed to amass in their rise-to-fame, only allowed them to build greater "walls" around their weaknesses, while those very weaknesses festered and grew into an "Achilles Heel". What usually results later is *a painful fall from glory*; drug, alcohol and substance abuse, domestically violent and abusive relationships, multiple visits to rehabilitation centers, bankruptcies, jail time, depression, failed marriages and suicides. The list goes on and on. Meanwhile, we withdraw our financial support. Destroy them on social media and blame them for not measuring up to the very standards that we never required of them to begin with. That's a heavy price to have to pay for not dealing with your *stuff*.

Word to the wise: Money, fame and fortune does not *fix* you, your issues, nor does it make you *better*. Money only has the power to make *you* more of who you *already are,* whatever state of mind you happen to be in. If you don't deal with your "Achilles Heel" now, it will take you down later. The longer you wait, the harder the crash. My advice: Confront it now. Burying or hiding it only gives it the power to grow into a bigger problem and then hurt you later.

Your <u>first</u> responsibility in life is to "grow up" on the *inside*, and by that I mean taking full ownership for that which you are responsible for: Your attitude, actions, character, values, choices and your future. Your strengths, talents and passions will only carry you so far in life, but what will sustain you is your character, values and vision. In this world, you had better know *who* you are, or it will allow you to rise and will watch you *fall* from the very glory it gives you. (We will work on this more in the next section).

Note: Buried weaknesses are like infected wounds that we cover with a bandage. Covering it up, does not fix it. The infection spreads to every part of your body. Ripping off the bandage of an infected wound never feels good and the longer it has been there, the less we prefer to deal with it. I will argue, however, that living with a growing infection feels even worse. Stop protecting it from the required treatment. Rip of the bandage and deal with it.

JUST BE YOURSELF. EVERYONE ELSE IS ALREADY TAKEN.

Opening note: Your strengths make you amazing, while your weaknesses make you human. The combination makes you lovable.

When did "being *ME*" become so difficult?

(Okay, prepare for this one… It's simple, but a big pill to swallow)… Here it is: Being YOU can at times feel difficult if you are still in your yet to be proven stage, which means that you have yet to receive the praise, popularity and positive feedback from other people just for being your authentic and wonderful *self*. That is why it may seem easier to try and imitate someone else who already appears to be popular or acceptable because whatever they are *doing* seems to be *working*.

Our very human nature tells us that if you want what *they* have, then we must start acting like they act and doing what they do. What results is a vain effort to imitate *that* person's style, their mannerisms, their slang, their walk, their 'swag' etc., especially if the results that they are getting are enviable. The problem with this is it creates resentment towards our authentic and underdeveloped selves and we end up taking on not just a few traits of the person we are imitating, rather more than we should, i.e. Not just the good stuff but the not so good stuff as well: (example: If they curse, then we feel like we need to curse. If they are disrespectful, we start to become disrespectful. If they jump off of a bridge…. You get the point. Don't sacrifice the potential of your authentic self for the temporary results that appear to be glorious.

Note: What people will ultimately admire about you is your genuine authenticity, not how well you imitated someone else. Popularity comes and goes, but authenticity lasts a lifetime.

I once had to decide that I am okay with not being the tallest, most athletic, most popular. When I learned to own this instead of fighting it, I started developing confidence. When I had confidence, people started taking an interest in who I was and I made friends so much easier. Ultimately, people want to associate with someone who doesn't feel like they have to follow the crowd (and in the middle of all this, I found out that I had a small talent for *speaking*... something that others would later come to admire me for. That talent and passion that I emitted, made people start to look past all of my flaws and insecurities and become interested in who I really was. Not who they wanted me to be and they absolutely looked over my weaknesses. That's when I started REALLY making friends. But I never would have gotten there had I not first LET GO of the approval addiction.

YOU

Are perfectly packaged for your "lane" in life, even with all of your brilliant imperfections. Therefore, own them without shame! Example: I am not as *tall* as I would like to be and it used to make me insecure. But I own that!

Note: Once I decided to embrace the height that I *do* have, I saw things much differently. I later stumbled upon some research and found out that I'm actually the *perfect height* to be casted as a character in movies! How great do you think you will feel when you make the conscious *choice* to *own* what you might believe to be imperfections? This is the very essence of *loving yourself*! People are naturally inspired by somebody who, in spite of their imperfections, is <u>confident</u> in their looks, their body, strengths, weaknesses and who does not feel the need to imitate other people! I learned that was the ultimate trick (formula): First, loving who you <u>are</u>. And then, being okay with who you are not!

Note: People who have 'unfollowed the crowd' love themselves, flaws and all! (Let's instead call these flaws: imperfections!)

Personally, I love the fact that I'm not *good at everything*. Quite frankly, there are some things that I absolutely struggle with and suck at! And that's okay. I own that! I really don't want to be good at *everything,* because quite frankly, I don't want to *do* everything!

Loving yourself will cause other people to respect you, look up to you and want to love themselves as well. Self-love is the best kind of confidence there is! These are people who will always acknowledge that they are not perfect and that they have their ups and downs. Self-love is about taking pride in your differences and your craft, protecting it, being honest about your weaknesses and shortcomings. Unapologetic about your strengths, your values and your standards. Own it!

Who's your *idol?*

Note: it is impossible to adequately duplicate someone else

It is always easier, of course, to do what's already been proven to be effective. Starting out, one of the hardest things to do, is be your authentic self, if you have yet to clearly define it. So imitating popular or successful others, is often easier... because they are already popular. They are already accepted and liked. So the psychology says, *"let me ditch who I am, forget about working on myself - and just copy someone else... so that I can be* <u>*liked*</u> *faster"*.

Here's the truth....You will never be good at being "somebody else", just as they could never duplicate you. You will only EVER be best at being yourself. If you make your goal to be like someone else, you will spend a lifetime consistently failing. There are so many messages out there about who to be and who to be. But whom will you choose to be? Everyone from rappers and artists to reality show stars displaying their standard of behavior, to models and media glorifying a certain standard of beauty, all have a way of making you feel like you'll never measure up to the standard - as you abuse yourself to fit into that proxy.

- *"When people are free to do as they please, they usually imitate each other"* - Eric Hoffer

Have you ever thought about what the world would be like, if EVERYONE looked just alike? It would be pretty boring. You are your own **unique self:** even if you're a twin. Let's take it a step further: have you ever wondered why you weren't born in another country or era? I am going to contend to say that it is because you weren't needed back then, rather now in present day. Walk with me on this... I am convinced, that there is no one else like you and there will never be another you ever again. There is something about your look, age, personality, talents and fabric being (once developed), that the world absolutely needs in this day and age... But think about it and consider, that THAT cannot happen if your entire focus is to try and change yourself to be someone "else".

Note: when you compare yourself to someone else, you're making them your idol

Not getting enough "Likes"?

Don't look to be understood by the world or live your life based on the validation of other people. The average person in the world only knows to trust that of which it knows to be popular, while humanity shy's away from what and whom it does not fully understand. Therefore, if you are still in that "unproven" stage, don't seek to be liked and accepted by everyone you come across. There are some that will, but most probably won't, and that's okay. Additionally, don't look for everyone to accept and like all of your bright ideas, jokes, stories, and the way you talk, think, speak or tie your shoes. We sometimes get caught up in the dilution of thinking that if we can become nice enough, cool enough, or just do enough "good" stuff, that we will be accepted by those whom we want to like us.

Consider this: Do not make it your mission in life to be "liked". That's too shallow. Your mission should be doing whatever it takes to get your best work into the world, so that humanity can be made better because you lived. Everyone will not like you for it, but those who will benefit will love you for it… (Understand and be okay with that). Think of every famous leader who has gone down in history for their greatness (Abraham Lincoln, Martin Luther King Jr, Winston Churchill). Most of them were hated before they were loved, but they understood that they had work to do in this world. Work that was far too important to worry about being "liked".

"Only 10 of them are guaranteed to *like* you"

Allow me to share with you some of the best advice I've ever received (as I was becoming a professional speaker). "*Jarrod, No matter how nice you are or how hard you try, there will always be someone that will not be a fan of yours. It's natural. In an audience full of people, 10-percent of them will love you no matter what! Even if you completely flop! Another 10-percent of the audience will dislike you no matter what you do! But that middle 80-percent is on you. They are the ones that are open to persuasion*". Wise words spoken to me by one of my phenomenal coaches, Josh Shipp. Let's apply this wisdom to *your* life. There will always be that percentage of people that will love you no matter what, and another percentage that may not approve of you no matter what you do or say! But that middle "80-percent" is open to your persuasion. That's your shot.

A little note: Even the perfect version of you will not be liked by EVERYBODY. That's the way it is supposed to be, and it's okay, but as you become confident in your authentic self, they will respect you.

They may not like it, but they will always respect your talent and authenticity.

Who do you WANT to be?

Imitation feels easy, but it's weak. The risk of being yourself is harder, but it's better. It's more rewarding. That is your killer combination and main advantage that you have over everyone else in the world.

What kind of person do you want to be known as?

_____

_____

_____

_____

NITTY GRITTY QUESTIONS: (Answer in Full)

What is your dream job and why?

_____

_____

_____

_____

Who is a successful individual, as an example, that is living the life that you most want to live:

_____

_____

_____

_____

What do you think it is like?

_____

_____

_____

_____

What are your talents? (*The things you excel at*)

Ex: *Speaking, Cooking, and Cleaning (the WAY you do something... If you just like doing it, then it may just be a passion)*

_____

_____

_____

_____

What are you best at? (Ps. *It doesn't matter if you think someone else is better at it*)

_____

_____

_____

_____

What kinds of problems or issues do people come to you for solutions on?

Ex. *Decorating ideas, hairstyle ideas,*

_____

_____

_____

_____

What kinds of things do people always ask you for help with?

_____

_____

_____

_____

What comes easy to you, but difficult to others?

_____

_____

_____

_____

What do YOU think needs _doing_ in today's world and why?

_____

_____

_____

_____

What is it that people least understand about you?

_____

_____

_____

_____

What is it that you wish people understood better about you?

_____

_____

_____

Are you willing to do something about that?

_____ (*yes or no*)

What is your favorite food?

_____

_____

_____

_____

What is your favorite TV show and why?

_____

_____

_____

_____

What is your favorite movie and why?

_____

_____

_____

_____

Who are your top 5 favorite music artists and why? Do they stand for something that resonates with you? Do their lyrics speak truth to you? Explain....

_____

_____

_____

_____

What issues anger you the most?

_____

_____

_____

When you are angry about an issue, what do you go and do about it?

_____

_____

_____

_____

I love it when...

_____

_____

_____

_____

I hate it when...

_____

_____

_____

_____

I get most excited when...

_____

_____

_____

_____

I am the most fulfilled when...

_____

_____

_____

What kinds of things do you get on your friends about all the time?

_____

_____

_____

_____

Interview your three most trusted friends (or family), to whom you believe best understand you. Ask them this: _What do YOU personally feel are my top strengths? What do you think I do best? What issues or problems would you personally come to ME with to help solve?_

Note: Make sure this is someone who you absolutely trust. Someone who will not criticize or "hate on you".

(List their answers here):

_____

_____

_____

_____

_____

_____

_____

_____

_____

_____

_____

_____

Do you feel that their answers were accurate?

_____

_____

_____

_____

Are the above items true strengths or real weaknesses?

_____

_____

_____

_____

I am honestly the worst when it comes to:

_____

_____

_____

_____

I am honestly right in my *zone* when it comes to:

_____

_____

_____

_____

I get frustrated when:

_____

_____

_____

_____

Describe your ideal work setting and the people that are there:

_____

_____

_____

_____

I am the most confident when I:

_____

_____

_____

_____

If you were paid $1,000,000.00 per year to do ANYTHING you wanted, what would you be doing with your life? (By the way, sleeping in, playing video games, vacationing, shopping and other forms of *entertainment* DO NOT count! Those are rewards and privileges for completed work. So what ELSE would you be doing with your life? Your greatest fulfillment will come from solving problems that your passions and strengths are an answer to). Write down what comes to mind:

_____

_____

_____

_____

_____

_____

_____

_____

_____

_____

_____

_____

_____

_____

_____

Describe your dream day in full detail: (What time would you wake up? Describe your future home? Describe your daily routine and to-do list. Describe your dream work. Write it out in full detail from start to finish**):**

_____

_____

_____

_____

_____

_____

_____

I feel most motivated when (or by):

_____

_____

_____

_____

_____

_____

_____

What kinds of people do you see yourself helping and serving?

_____

_____

_____

_____

What is your favorite book and why?

_____

_____

_____

_____

What three things would you go and do right now if you knew there was no way that you could fail? (And why?)

_____

_____

_____

_____

_____

_____

_____

_____

_____

_____

_____

What one thing can you commit to doing about one of those above items right now?

_____

_____

_____

_____

I totally believe in (and why):

Ex. *Educating oneself. Getting all the facts before speaking*

_____

_____

_____

_____

I am totally against (and why):

Ex. ignorance

_____

_____

_____

_____

If you only had 100 days left to live and make an impact on this world, what would you be doing with your life? (If you could achieve ANYTHING within these 100 days, what would it be?)

_____

_____

_____

_____

_____

_____

_____

Fast forward to the end of your life. As a result of your having lived, list at least three things that you did that changed the world, or at least someone's world for the better:

_____

_____

_____

_____

_____

_____

How do you want the world to remember you?

_____

_____

_____

_____

_____

_____

More than *anything* else in the world, I really want to:

_____

_____

_____

_____

(Let's talk *Character*): What are your morals?

_____

_____

_____

_____

What are your boundaries? What nonsense do you

Refuse to allow to come into your life?

_____

_____

_____

_____

I totally stand for:

_____

_____

_____

I am completely against:

_____

_____

_____

_____

What are your values?

_____

_____

_____

_____

What one thing do you love so much that you would do it for free?

_____

_____

_____

_____

Who are the adults that you respect the most? The ones you are afraid to disappoint?

_____

_____

_____

What is the greatest vision that you have for your life?

_____

_____

_____

_____

_____

_____

_____

What will be your legacy?

_____

_____

_____

Name just ONE thing that you can go and do about it TODAY:

_____

_____

_____

YOU ARE A
CELEBRITY

Which means that we all mean something to someone, and seldom do we understand the depth and extent of our value and impact. There is always someone that is watching you, looking up to you, admiring you, even if for something small, whether you realize it or not. That is an opportunity to make an impact on someone's life! Don't take that opportunity lightly.

Simply put: Before you "pull the trigger" (like we talked about earlier), please understand that you mean *something* to *someone* and that should mean everything to you. We all bring a special something into this world and share it with others, yet we seldom understand what that "thing" is or how great the impact. Here's why: You've lived with *yourself* your entire life, which means you don't always recognize that you have a unique way of saying things and doing things that make a certain impact. Because it's completely natural to you, you may not recognize the gift as easily as others who have benefited from it will. You are a unique beast!

"To the wrong person you'll never have any worth, but to the right person, you'll mean everything" - "Pastor Dave" (God's not Dead, 2014)

ROCK YOUR ONE TALENT

The Role You Play

Let's shift gears here. While everyone on the planet has strengths and innate abilities, many of the greatest talents come in the form of inner attributes that are often overshadowed and go unnoticed. Here's what I mean: When we hear the word *talent*, we often get distracted by thinking it needs to be something overly obvious, like: Dancing, singing, twirling a baton, figure skating or painting a Picasso. While you very well may excel in these areas, please understand that most people's greatest attributes are actually more mute and underdeveloped, but have the greatest impact.

Maybe *yours* is researching, idea generating, creative writing, styling, making difficult-to-understand things easier to understand, teaching, assisting others, always having a great attitude, being an encourager, strong leadership, thinking before you speak, conflict resolution, showing compassion, persuasion, organization, following instructions, fixing things that are broken or tinkering with things to make them better. Other times, the very thing you do best (the thing you do naturally), that annoys other people could end up being *the thing* you get paid to do as a career (plenty of world class comedians were initially class-clowns who were kicked out of class every other day of the week).

What are some of the silent attributes that come natural for you? What effect do you tend to have on other people? What do you bring to the *table*?

_____

_____

_____

_____

Note: As you write this exercise, you will begin to see more of what it is that others in fact value you for and appreciate the role you play. You will begin to understand your value in certain relationships, organizations and environments. You will come to understand more about who you are and love *yourself* even more in the process.

Rock Your One *Talent*

By now, you should have successfully identified a few strengths and attributes. While I want you to feed your interests and be involved in as many extracurricular activities as you can get your hands on, I am going to encourage you in this: Out of all the things that you do well, you should focus on doing at least *one* thing phenomenally well, above everything else. Personally, rather than being known for being good at *everything*, I would rather be known for doing *one* thing insanely well! And then maybe be known for being *pretty* good at a few other things.

Cheap Advice: *"Don't put all your eggs in one basket"*

Argument: *"But what if I only have one basket"*?

Truth: You have several baskets.

Wisdom: Fill the largest basket with the most eggs first. That basket would be labeled: *"My Greatest Strength"*.

"But I'm not good at anything"

Not true! Everyone is good at *something*. It just takes time, practice and exercise to become great at that *something*. I am willing to bet that whatever it is, you are probably already doing it and overlooking it, for the sake of it not being the overly obvious talent that you might have hoped to be flaunting in life.

True Story

Back in high school, I had a friend named Elizabeth. A very kind and fun person. She seemed to be the "girl next door", except she was known for doing one thing better than anyone else in school: She had a phenomenal singing voice. Anytime our school needed someone to sing the national anthem at a sports game or a musical performer for a production, they would hunt her down. I remember one time we were standing around after class having a conversation with a teacher and another student. The student asked Elizabeth: 'Have you always had this gift for singing'?

Elizabeth gave a response that surprised all of us. In her own words: 'No. Definitely not! When I was younger, I didn't have a singing voice at all, but I always knew I wanted to be a singer. So I just took my favorite song and I sang it over and over and over until I started to notice improvement. Everyone would always tell me to shut up; my brothers, sisters… Even my parents! None of them liked my voice, and everyone thought I was being annoying. But I never stopped singing. It had always been a passion and over time I noticed that the more I practiced, the stronger my voice became, the easier it was to hit notes, perform chord modulations and sound how I wanted to sound. Now, every time I take the stage to sing, I feel as if I've arrived and am doing what I was always meant to do…. And I'm still a work in progress!'

Here was someone that the entire student body celebrated for a talent that they thought she was simply born with. It was not given. It was earned. What we had been admiring was her passion and determination against the criticisms and those who tried to make her shrink back. Everyone has a passion. Once you find it, focus on it and build on it until it becomes a talent, then a skill and then search for opportunities where it can be utilized. This is how you *arrive*!

Note: If you want something badly enough, go get it. Some talents can be <u>earned</u>.

What is it that comes easy to you but difficult to everyone else? What kinds of things do others appreciate about you that you don't think are a big deal? Better yet, what kinds of things are you passionate about that you haven't applied the proper time and energy towards making happen? Is it possible that maybe, like Elizabeth, you too have a phenomenal talent within but have been too lazy to put in the time and effort? Maybe you have invested *some* time and *some* effort, but have you stuck with it long enough and consistently enough to see how great you could possibly be at it? If not... Then get started!

Note: It's so much easier when you can just focus on ONE thing and really MASTER it! Don't be afraid to play the "one-string on your guitar".

THE TRUTH ABOUT MISTAKES

Note: It's much easier to "go to school" on someone *else's* mistakes. Please learn from mine.

Just ONE of the biggest mistakes I have ever made…

I once wrote a death threat to someone who I called my best friend. Her name is Kayla. She and I grew up together in the same neighborhood and have known each other ever since we were small enough to take bubble baths together as toddlers. As kids, we spent our entire summers playing together, catching fireflies together, riding our bikes together, swimming in the pool together, eating dinner at each other's houses together and always getting into trouble together. I can't remember a time in our lives when we didn't know one another. Where she went, I went, and vice versa. We spent what felt like every waking moment of our childhood *together*. We were two 'peas in a pod'.

As we approached middle school, however, all of that suddenly changed. I grew to "like" her as more than a friend, however, something else in the realm of our relationship *shifted*. I watched her become absorbed into a new friendship circle and we began to grow apart. We stopped hanging out around each other, calling one another or talking. For whatever reason, she resorted to spreading rumors about me, convincing others not to like me, hang around me or talk to me. For what seemed like no good reason at all, I felt as if she was deliberately alienating me from her life all together, while convincing others to do the same (and was enjoying it). We had somehow gone from being the best of confidants to somewhat enemies.

My transition that year from elementary into middle school was less than ideal. I did not adjust well with the new style of classroom learning or with my new classmates and was bullied quite a bit. That same year my older brother, whom I was close with and could always talk to about anything, had graduated high school and enlisted in the Navy where he would be stationed overseas for three-years with limited communication. My dad, who lived an hour away had remarried, and preferred that I didn't come for visits for a while because they had just given birth to my baby sister and needed time to adjust. When I was able to come around, I no longer had a bedroom but had to sleep in the basement. With so many fast changes, alienation, stress from school and feelings of abandonment and hurt, I became bitter, angry and identified Kayla as the person holding the 'straw that broke the camel's back'.

Note: People you love and care about are still human and may just disappoint you, hurt you and abandon you. In such cases, the only thing you are responsible for is how you will respond.

It was the one of the dumbest, most irresponsible, cowardice and hateful choices I have ever made in my life. I decided that because Kayla had hurt me that I had to hurt her back. I pulled out some paper and I wrote to her an anonymous letter, spawned out of hate. I penned all of the anger that I felt towards her, telling her that she was going to *be sorry* and that she would die.

-    *"When you get emotional, you get stupid." - Dave Ramsey*

Late that night, around 1 o'clock in the morning, I snuck out of my mom's house for the first time, to deliver the letter to Kayla's mailbox down the street. I had memorized where all the creeks in the floor were and avoided them as I snuck out, "stealth-ninja" style, as to not wake my mom.

There I was, in the middle of the night, on my down the street to Kayla's house. My heart was beating heavily at the thought of my devious plan. Understanding the possibility of being caught at any moment, I contemplated turning back. But my emotions and rage made me unafraid of the consequences. I was a "terrorist" on my way to exact my revenge and somebody was going to pay. I went ahead with it. I <u>committed</u>.

Note: Your emotions are your enemy.

As I got closer to her driveway, I carefully studied the house to make sure all of the lights were off. I remembered her having a squeaky mailbox, so I would have to be careful, quiet and efficient. I managed to quietly drop the note in their mailbox next to the front door, tiptoed my way off of her front porch and ran back down the street to my house as fast as humanly possible. My heart pounded heavily in my chest as I laid in bed that night, feeling a bit of fear and guilt from the thought of the sequence of events that would ignite from my choice, but feeling mildly justified at the pain that someone else was going to endure for what they did to me.

The next day…

Unable to get over my hurt feelings, I didn't just write one letter. I wrote several, and at least two more over the week following the original. After the third letter, word and panic began to spread around our school, that someone was 'trying to kill' Kayla. I remember walking past her one day while she stood at her locker with one of the letters in her hands. Out of the corner of my eye I remember seeing her surrounded by several of her friends who were each in amazement at the very prospect that she could be in real danger. Bringing her physical harm was of course the last thing I would have ever done, but there was certainly a twisted 'high' that I was getting from watching the person that hurt me begin to suffer.

Kayla's mom was a teacher at our middle school and wanted nothing more than to get to the bottom of the issue, wisely suspecting that the perpetrator was someone "close to home". Over the next few days, she had delivered the letters to our school administration who took the threat very seriously and later commissioned the school's security guards to take writing samples of every student in order to try and get a match on the letter's originator.

This had become pretty serious.

The death threats were, for a while, the most talked about subject at our school and they were determined to catch the person responsible. Fearing that I would be exposed, I did the next logical thing I could think of: *run from it. Hide from it.* I had even gone as far as to lead them in the direction of a few other 'potential suspects'.

I managed to avoid being fingerprinted or questioned by security, as hundreds of other kids in my school were also left untested. Ultimately there were just too many people in our school to be able to go through all of us, much less sustain an accurate investigation of this length. When choosing *revenge,* you may *feel* like you're getting even, but in our doing so we often neglect the reality that we still have to sleep at night and have peace of mind. I had neither. Peace or rest. Eventually the thought of how scared or hurt Kayla might be, began to eat away at me. Here is someone who I actually loved and cared about. I couldn't believe that I had brought myself to do something on this scale, no matter how much I thought she hurt me. Eventually, Kayla got past it and everyone moved on, except me. Nothing got better. It wasn't worth it.

"The monks used to say that revenge is like a two-headed rat-viper. While you watch your enemy go down, you're being poisoned yourself." - Avatar Aang

Note: When you have something painful or embarrassing in your life, don't run from it. FIX it. Because until you do, it's just poison in your body. You won't be a real man or woman until you can tell the truth about your lies and secrets. *That's* the healing part.

We went all throughout middle school, high school and college without my saying a word in regards to the famed 'death threat' letters. We had managed to become friends again and although it has now been more than ten-years since the incident, I recently found the courage to face the issue, admit it to her, and apologize sincerely. It was one of the hardest thing I've ever had to do, as a guy, to become vulnerable and admit the truth about my past weakness and the series of choices I made because of it. Weaknesses and choices that I had constructed 'walls' around. Back then, I had made it up in my mind that this would just be one of those things that I would go to my grave with and never uncover.

As I reached out to her and told her the truth, it was as if the weight of the world had lifted off of my shoulders. A weight that I didn't even know was there. Even though it has been more than a decade, this one little thing in my past, was still an issue that would still come up in my heart every now and then. Although it no longer mattered to her. I was no longer hiding. No longer held hostage by a secret. What I'm really saying here is: don't be a victim of your past. If the issue is still in your heart *somewhere*, have the courage to be a real man or woman and address it, fix it and move on, no matter how you think the other person might respond. The added benefit to this is Kayla really didn't care! We caught up with one another, had some laughs and she forgave me instantly.

I share this story with you, because as elementary as it may be and as ancient as the incidents were, it's the little unresolved things that have a way of playing out in your life years later. It reflects in your confidence, performance, attitude, thoughts, beliefs, self-esteem and more.

Note: When you're afraid to do something that you know you *should* do, the way you become more courageous is by <u>committing</u> to just *doing* at least one thing, that you don't <u>think</u> you have the courage to do. Courage, strength and power will meet you at the point of execution! The key here, is YOU must commit <u>first</u> in order for the courage to come. It will show up for you when needed.

Just *'be a man!'*

I believe that if you are a mature human being, whether male or female, you don't run from your problems. You face them, you step up and DO something about what's bothering you in your life. You don't blame someone else for why you did something nor do you create a wall of excuses to negate your actions. If you are mature you just own it and take responsibility. As long as you're trying to justify the wrong that you did, then you are not truly repentant or sorry about it. You're still being a victim which is the same as *choosing* to be weak.

Who's *really* the guilty party?

Did you know that in many cases dealing with school-wide *bullying*, the person who is found to be 'guilty' is not the one who committed the first offense or throws the first punch? The guilty party is often the victim who chooses to respond with a counter attack. In life, people are going to hurt you, disappoint you, talk about you, 'hate on you', alienate you and bully you. Some will become jealous of you and even try their hardest to bring you down. Who are you going to be when it's time to do something about it?

Note: Refuse, at all costs, to operate in your "lower" nature: Hate, anger and revenge. For those things will only poison *you* in the long run, and that is way too much energy, focus and commitment to give to someone who wants to eliminate you.

A *real* Man or Woman: Understands who he or she really is. They have taken careful inventory of their morals, standards and identity. They stand up for what is right and for what they believe in, even when it's not popular. They do not run from their problems or look to get even. They are the same person of integrity in public as they are when behind 'closed doors'. They aren't afraid to apologize when they're wrong and they assume the courage to own up for whatever they are responsible for, their choices and the <u>mistakes</u> they have made (whether they were made intentionally or unintentional).

FIX your messes

Even if it is nothing more than a sincere apology for something you were involved in. You will never know how long you've been suffering with it until you *step-up*. Ownership of the role you may have played in a situation, even if you weren't completely at fault, can set you completely <u>free</u> from the seed of festering guilt and future blame from others. *Owning-up* does not mean that you are accepting fault or taking all of the blame for something, rather you're acknowledging that the other person may have suffered something at *your hand*, and are committing to doing what you can to help resolve what could be a difficult matter.

But do I *have* to?

No. But you should. Here's why: Sickness, poor health, fatigue, low energy, worry and guilt will all be lying dormant in your body, slowly making you sick, until you decide to step up. This is what I call: *'Suicide the slow-way'*. But once you <u>commit</u>, own it, correct it, apologize or make up for it, you're officially free from it. Regardless of how the other person may feel about it. Even if the person you have to apologize to becomes angry or upset, don't let that uncomfortable thought of potentially losing the relationship, stop you from doing what is right.

They will usually take the truth of your confession better than you may think. Conversely, when someone wrongs *you*, be quick to forgive them as well. Forgiving them does not mean that you are forgetting everything they have done. It means that you refuse to carry around anger, vengeful feelings, resentment or bitterness in your mind, heart and body. The very things that kill you. On the other hand, if they come to you, admit their wrong, then please accept that they did it out of their heart and because they value their relationship with you, no matter what the circumstances are or how bad the offense was. Forgive!

More WISDOM: When you have someone at your mercy, show mercy! Refuse to hold them hostage to your un-forgiveness! You will be freeing them from the guilt that is eating them alive from the inside. Liberate them from that through your forgiveness. To them, you will always be known as the person that set them free them from their pain. You will feel great about it and they will become a loyal and lifelong ally.

Note: Leave your past right where it is! (IN the past). Ever made a mistake? I have made several! You are not your painful past nor are you the mistakes that you have made (even if the mistake was one that you made today!). Sometimes, when you've done something reprehensible in life, it will be in the very nature of people to label you according to their experience with you. It is not uncommon for insecure people to label you according to their hurt (example: *"Once a liar, always a liar. Once a cheater, always a cheater."*). Oftentimes they will want to categorize you for the way they remember you having been, because it feels comfortable and safe for the moment. They have fooled themselves into believing that as long as they stay mad at you, that they are making you pay for whatever it is that you did. The truth of the matter is, *they* are the only ones paying the price: (anger, hurt and resentment robs people of their peace).

The BEST teachers!

No matter what age you are (whether you're seven-years old or seventy-years old), people who have made mistakes and <u>own</u> them are the <u>best teachers</u>, because they have *lived* it. They can teach the lesson from a real life perspective. They can show you the intricate *in's and out's.* They can talk about the mindset behind it, the reasonings, the excuses and transitions. They understand how it felt to once hide their issues out of weakness and insecurity. They also understand the feeling of self-vindication because they have walked every step of the path to freedom and peace. They can relate to you better and are qualified to offer counsel as you experience yours. They are credible because they have lived on both sides of it. Let your "owned" mistakes be like educational degrees that you received in those areas. Conversely, a mistake you ran from, is a test that you failed and are afraid to make-up.

Note: Do not be afraid of the make-up test. The biggest mistakes are those you refuse to learn from.

The Truth About Regrets:

Mistakes are natural and necessary for growth. However, if you are carrying regret and sorrow about something that you have done in your past, don't! In my book, regrets are nothing more than excuses. A regret means that you have convinced yourself that you have zero power to do anything about your situation. That is a grand deception my friend! You always have the power to take action!

Most people will go to great lengths to cover up their mistakes (build "walls") due to embarrassment and pride. Don't play that game. Own your stuff! The goal in life is not to see how perfect you can be or how few times you can mess up. You're supposed to take some calculated risks and possibly stumble. Even if at times it was done purposely to test the limits. That's how we grow. Even as you matured through your childhood development stages, part of your job was to test the limits by challenging authority.

Here's what I mean…

Growing up as a toddler, do you remember your parents telling you what your first word was? Every toddler's first word spoken will obviously be different from everyone else', but it is a proven fact, that at least one of the first five learned words of every human being, is "no".

I'm not telling you to go out in the world and deliberately make mistakes. That would be unwise. To willfully make a bad choice is called *being an idiot*, undisciplined, or at the very least: emotionally immature. True, the decision to repeat a mistake is called a bad choice, nonetheless, don't be so hard on yourself. Give yourself time to fix your mistakes and grow. Allow your authentic mistakes to serve as little hallmarks in your life that show you what to do differently *next time* and the things that you will remember *not to do!* The reward here is a reserve of priceless wisdom that you can draw from, rely on, teach and pass along in your legacy. Mistakes, once put in this perspective, will help you to become who you *are*.

Say this aloud with me: (with power, passion and conviction):

"Mistakes are natural. I make mistakes, but I am NOT a mistake. My mistakes do not make me dumb, stupid or less than smart. They are only the result of a misunderstanding and some wisdom that I lacked that would only be earned through the price of a mistake. My mistakes are only there to help me grow into a smarter and wiser human being and teacher of life. With every mistake, I become smarter, wiser, and more confident and grow into a phenomenal human being with value, power and unlimited potential. I choose not hide from my mistakes, or cover them up, or protect them, or make

excuses for them, or lie about them or build up walls around them. I am honest with myself. I own my mistakes and the lessons they teach me. I take full responsibility for my life and my actions whether they are intended or unintended. I am in control of my life, my words and my choices - for THAT is the mark of a real man / woman."

A little note on how to treat people: People will never remember everything that you said to them but they will <u>always</u> remember how you made them <u>feel</u>. If their last encounter with you was negative, that is how you will be remembered for treating them and that is how they will most likely speak of you when given the opportunity. But when you share your heart by apologizing, showing compassion and kindness, you will change their memory of you from negative to positive.

The reason that this is so powerful:

People's <u>words</u>, both written and spoken make a <u>huge</u> difference in your life. Words, once spoken actually happen (I will prove this). Have you ever called someone a name or been called a name? One of my many jobs is as a teacher-trainer (as young as I am, I am actually certified to travel the nation and train large groups of teachers on how to have better relationships with their students, by doing most of the stuff I am teaching you to do in this book!). One of the many complaints that I receive from teachers is that their students never turn in their work on time, that they don't care about anything and that they *never* 'pull up their pants'.

During one such seminar, after a careful line of questioning, I asked a few of them to share with me what *they DO* about being frustrated at their students'. In my own words: *"What do you <u>say</u> to them? How exactly do you respond?"* Their answers absolutely shocked me! These teachers admitted to resorting to anger, frustration and yelling. Telling their students: *"You all are so disrespectful! You're* *always late*, you *never turn your work in on-time*, *you don't care about anything*, and *you never pull up your pants!"*

I thanked each of them for sharing and then asked them the *million-dollar question: "Well if these are the labels you are giving them, and the names you are calling them, then why are you surprised when they are living them out?"* The room fell silent. The truth is, when a person hears you call them a name long enough, sooner or later they will have no choice but to record it in their subconscious (which is the part of the brain that programs us for *auto-pilot*) and live that name out. Eventually, that classroom of students that have been called *disrespectful*, blamed for: *not caring about anything, turning in their homework late and never pulling up their pants,* will ultimately become those very things.

Note: <u>What is spoken is real</u>. Words give the subconscious mind instructions on what to do. Once those words have been spoken enough times, they are recorded in the subconscious and ready to be carried out through one's actions, thoughts and choices. Never give yourself or someone else a label or a name that you <u>do not</u> want them or yourself to become. **You do NOT have to <u>be</u> the labels other people have given you.**

If something someone said to you in fact hurt you, I am willing to bet that there was already some insecurity inside of you that their words just happened to *trigger*. When you feel that anger, hurt, guilt, embarrassment or shame based on someone else's words, here's what you do: Own it. Here's how: When you can, go somewhere where you can be in solitude and say these words to yourself: *"I <u>admit</u> that what (<u>person's NAME</u>) said to me in fact <u>hurt</u> me. Their words spoke against the very nature of whom <u>I really am</u> and want to be in life. They stumbled over one of <u>my</u> weaknesses that I have been hiding. One that I am still sensitive about and have yet to fully overcome. Today, <u>I choose to own</u> that weakness and* _commit to doing_ at least one thing about it, starting by confronting it (the weakness). I forgive (_person's name_) for what they said to me, and as I work on my weakness today, I am gaining strength and feel peace. Because I have _committed_ to this process, I will win! I feel better already!" (Repeat this over and over until you begin to feel better)

If you have been given a label or a name that is unfair or causing you to think, act or be something that you shouldn't then you can change it! Decide who you _do_ want to be and start saying _that_ every time you feel the opposite way. It works just the same as above. Once you have said it enough times, you will begin to believe it is real. You will act differently, choose differently and get better results.

Questions: What names or labels have you been given that now cause you to think the way you think, act the way you act, choose the way you choose or do the things you do? What have you been "programmed" to do?

"I am a machine!" - (Terminator 3: Rise of The Machines, 2003)

In relation to the topic at hand, this dialogue below is taken from one of my favorite movie scenes of all time. We witness John Connor intensely pleading with the Terminator machine that was originally programmed to protect him, but now found itself turning on him. Read on (with my commentaries), and then we'll talk about it!

(Scene)

John: _[Sees Terminator coming towards plane] Yes, he made it!_

Terminator: _Get away from me! Leave... now!_

Kate: _[From plane] Let's go, John! [John hops into plane while Kate runs startup checklist] The master's on. Throttle's set._

John: *C'mon, let's go!* [Terminator yanks door open, grabs John, and throws him across the room. Terminator comes after him] *Please, you can't do this!*

This next line is <u>everything</u>:

Terminator: *I have no choice. The...T-X...has cor...Corrupted my system.*

John: *You can't kill a human being. You said so yourself!*

Kate: *[jumps on Terminator's back] Let him go! [Terminator throws her off]*

John: *You're fighting it right now!*

Terminator: *My CPU is intact. But I cannot control...my other functions.*

John: *You don't have to do this. You don't want to do this!!!*

Terminator: *Desire is irrelevant. I am a machine! [Grabs John and throws him against a car. Comes up and takes John by the throat]*

John: *What is your mission?!*

Terminator: *To ensure the survival of John Connor and Katherine Brewster. [Raises fist]*

John: *You are about to fail that mission!*

Terminator: *I can ... I cannot.*

John: *You know what you have to do!*

(End Scene)

Autopilot: A cognitive state in which you act without "self-awareness".

Words, when spoken, send instructions to your subconscious mind about who to be and how to be. When something is said to you time and time again, your subconscious mind (which is your internal autopilot) is now programmed with instructions to carry out. There are times where you will catch yourself behaving a certain way and not understand why. These are all effects of subconscious programming through words. What is spoken is indeed real.

Of course, this was just an illustration to heighten the main point, but what I most appreciate about this scene is the power of spoken words. We find John Connor pinned against the hood of a car by the Terminator, who is programmed and prepared to smash John's head into the engine, and then something amazing happens. He asks the Terminator one simple question: *"What is your mission?"* The Terminator responds: *"To ensure the survival of John Connor and Katherine Brewster".* Albeit he is a machine, that depiction speaks perfectly to our very human nature! Once the Terminator spoke those words, his "subconscious" was reprogrammed with a different set of instructions that proved powerful enough to override the previous programming. What a life lesson for the rest of us humans!

Note: *You* too have the power to override *the programming!*

Homework:

Consider the mistakes you have made in life. The labels that you've been given. The names that you've been called. The hurtful experiences that have been invited upon you. Now, I want you to consider what you want to be known for. Who you really want to become. The positive change that you wish to inject into the world to make it a better place. Your legacy. Fill in the blanks below and recite the phrases to yourself aloud daily! This is one of the fastest and easiest ways to create change in your personal life, by changing the "programming".

Secret: Whatever you put behind the words "I AM", will indeed give yourself instructions on what to become! So be VERY careful what you write!

In spite of my mistakes in life or the labels that were given me, I AM: _____

I love my ability to: _____

The entire world is waiting on me to show up! And I am going to change the world when I: _____

Despite anything that I have done, or the experiences that have taught me to back down, I will confidently take bold action and move forward in the direction of my dreams and goals, in spite of fear or rejection.

AGE DOES NOT MATTER

When you understand, decide, and <u>commit</u> to being who you are and the kind of person you desire to become, your age and a whole lot of other things <u>won't matter</u>. Maturity and achievement has nothing to do with being a certain age. It is about the choices you decide to make right where you are. You can "grow up" and make an impact in this world at any time that you decide to. Obtaining several college degrees and multi-billionaire status is not required in order to make a <u>difference</u>. You may be grounded in thinking that you are still too young to be able to do anything "big" or worthwhile. Realistically, you may require the help of several others, depending on the size of your goal or the impact you want to make, but consider this…

Note: When the student is ready, help will appear. It's all about your level of <u>commitment</u>. Being ready has nothing to do with money, support or smarts. It is simply an attitude that says: *"I see something that needs to be done and <u>I must do something</u> about it… right now."*

I remember meeting a 10-year old kid last year named Tanner. He told me an inspiring story about being 8-years old when he was volunteering his Saturday mornings to help serve meals to the homeless people within his inner-city community. He said that the issue of hunger in his community was one that he felt he must do something about. Without considering his young age or few resources, he immediately got a few of his friends together from school and decided to create a community service group that would feed the homeless every Saturday morning (with the help of a few adults of course). The first Saturday, the group pooled all of their allowance money and bought bread and ingredients from the grocery store. At 5:30am the group was busy at work in the kitchen at Tanner's house, where they would make over one-hundred peanut butter and jelly sandwiches. Later that morning they were able to feed at least one-hundred people.

This continued on for a few Saturdays. Eventually, the principal at their school thought it would be a great idea to try and get more students and families involved. To make a long story short, Tanner's passion for feeding people, attracted hundreds of people from the community to invest in his movement which now allows him to feed thousands of people in need every weekend. This community movement attracted the attention of local politicians and a few national celebrities who now also support his movement via word of mouth, supplies and media. Tanner has since been featured in several magazines, has been requested to speak at several national youth events and is highly celebrated for being a young leader in his community… all at the age of ten!

Note: You are never too young to just get started. Not once did Tanner talk himself out of his dreams because of his young age. He never created excuses for why he couldn't do what was in his heart to do for his community. The only special thing about Tanner was his willingness to ignore all of the obvious excuses that he could have made to never start. He just decided that something needed to be done about a problem he saw in his community, and did it! Never be discouraged by small beginnings. What began as a small kitchen operation with peanut butter and jelly (purchased on allowance-money), soon transformed into a mini empire that helps thousands of people and garners national media attention. You do not have to be older, richer or more educated to take action on your passions or convictions. There is always something that you can do right now! There is nothing stopping you except your own excuses for why you may think you can't.

Note: You can hold on to your dreams, ideas or plans until you think they are perfect or you can release what you have now and see what happens.

WARNING: <u>All</u> ideas come with an expiration date. So get moving! What you <u>won't</u> do, someone else <u>will</u> do. You will loathe and regret the day you see someone else living the dream you originally had, but refused to do anything about (or the dream you could have stuck with _long enough_ to see it grow). It will eat away at you. It will be a battle to refrain yourself from criticizing the other person for all of the things that they could be doing better, yet you won't be able to escape the reality that _you_ should have taken action on the idea when you had it! Don't let this be <u>you</u>. Don't sit back and wait until you have "more" talent, "more" personality or "more" courage. Just get started and everything you need will start to appear!

Who are your "_investors_"?

When on the road to achieving big goals and dreams, don't worry about where the help will come from. When you get moving on your positive passions, many people, friends and _investors_ will begin to appear on your path to help you, give you their best advice, sharpen you, coach you past your self-imposed limitations and push you to be your best. The process of sharpening may not always _feel_ good but it is always profitable. A good _investor_ will let you know when your efforts need to be better and they may often require you to do extra work. There may be times where you have to say "no" to a lot of distractions: TV, entertainment or things you may want to do, in order to do what you should do, so that you can become who you need to become. But the end results are phenomenal! Who have been your coaches, your support and teachers in life? An _investor_ can be anyone.

Here are just a few of mine:

When I finally <u>committed</u> to winning my first speech competition along came:

Mr. Spagnuolo ("Spag")

My A.P Literature teacher whose passion for teaching made us all want to learn. He worked with me for several days after school to help me perfect the winning speech that helped me earn first place in a state-wide competition.

When I finally <u>committed</u> to going to college along came:

Ms. Watkins

My neighbor who was also a high school teacher. She made me and one of my friends sit in her living room after school one day. She fed us and wouldn't let us leave until we applied for 50 college scholarships each. I earned a two year scholarship to the university of my choice and was given over $10,000.00 in monetary gifts from family, neighbor's teachers and other awesome adults that I had never even met! (Thank you all again btw!)

When I finally decided to stand up for myself in life along came:

Donnie & John

My two older cousins (like brothers) who showed me the proverbial "ropes" in life, taught me not to let people "walk all over me" and how to stand up for myself. They would even make me do pushups, lift weights, play tackle football and toughen up. They taught me to *hold my own* and made it their mission to get me ready for the world!

And there are many more…

KEY: When you commit the right help will arrive!

WISDOM: Someone who really loves you will make an *investment* in you with no guarantees. This is the very nature of <u>true love</u>.

My advice: *Don't fight the investor. You need them more than they need you.* I will remember these people for the rest of my life for the phenomenal human beings that they are and for the deposits they made into my life. Who are yours? What did they teach you? What deposits have they made in your life?

Investor 1: _____

Investor 2: _____

Investor 3: _____

Investor 4: _____

Investor 5: _____

Investor 6: _____

Investor 7: _____

Investor 8: _____

Investor 9: _____

Investor 10: _____

Note: The help is always there! They are just waiting to see if you have the heart to <u>commit</u>. As long as you are willing to invest in yourself, they will show up to invest in you too. No one ever gets anywhere, achieves a dream or does anything truly worthwhile that the world admires if they are afraid to take action. Don't be a pansy!

"People who have achieved their dreams just took 'the <u>leap</u>'… and built their wings on the way down" - Me

Return the love

Reflect on the people who have believed you, supported you, and saw potential in you at a time that you had yet to fully realize or appreciate it; someone who pushes you to be better. You may have one person in mind or maybe several. If they are still alive and you have access, write them a thank you, or tell them in person (you can even get creative and make video if you choose).

Every single one of us has someone like this in our lives. These are the caring individuals who are ready and willing to invest their time, wisdom and resources into us. These are the people who want nothing more than to see us grow into our greatest potential and require from us nothing in return (but they pray that you will become someone great). If the person you have in mind is no longer living, then pen your gratitude to them on paper or in a journal. You are not required to do anything special with the letter from there. You can put it away and save it, or shred it. However, just the act of writing your thoughts and thanks is a soul cleansing exercise that will bring about a greater level of peace in your daily walk.

Is it a teacher, mentor, counselor, pastor, family member or a friend? Sometimes that person is 'right under your nose' and won't be revealed until you first commit to something. Commit yourself to being better in some way. Commit yourself to a challenge, a goal, something that's bigger than yourself. Something that will require you to have help in order to finish strong, and then get to work! When you truly commit, the *investors* will always appear. When the goal is achieved, find those *investors* and thank them.

Commitment: *Make it up in your mind, that regardless of your limitations or the help that you don't have, that you are going to start your goal and finish your goal even if no one else comes along to help.*

Note: The best way to show gratitude to these kinds of people is by nurturing the seed they planted within you. Strive to become the best version of yourself that you possibly can.

"I'm looking at you and I see two people: You and a better you. Are you willing to work on it?" - Kevin Bracy

YOUR MISSION, SHOULD YOU CHOOSE TO ACCEPT IT

I want you to reflect on your the answers that you bravely provided earlier in the "Identity" section. The very answers you wrote down indeed reflect your identity, your truth and your reality. If there is anything that you do not like about the answers you wrote down and sincerely want to change those realities, you can! Imagine and ponder the <u>kind of person</u> that you *want* to become and be known for and then add that into your answers (or change some of the answers if you wish).

Now it's time to combine some of these answers and draft your very own Mission Statement. I have provided mine below to help you get started. Yours can be 20-pages long or one page long. That's up to you! :-). Notice your individuality and uniqueness. You may be just like a lot of other people in *some* areas, but no one has the exact same "combination" as anyone else or can effectively be *you* as well as you can. Take pride in being different. Embrace your uniqueness. It will serve you well!

Once you finish writing your mission statement, I want you to <u>commit</u> to it by signing it at the bottom of the page. Read it in the morning before you begin your day and before you go to bed. Say it aloud! This is what will help you to reprogram your subconscious from any negative programming that you have acquired in life. Place your sheet somewhere that is visible to you. I keep mine on my phone and tablet for quick reference. The more I learn, grow and change, the more adjustments I make to my mission statement. You will enjoy doing the same.

Note: The Mission Statement is a declaration designed to "program" you into the kind of person you want to become so that you can go forth to do the "big things" you want to do in life! Some of the statements you will write down should scare you (just a bit), because you are calling yourself higher than where you already are. So if you are someone who has always been afraid and have lacked courage, you might write and say: *"Even though I have resorted to running and hiding in the past, I am a confident, bold and fearless person! I carefully calculate my winning strategies and I always step up! I always do things that take more courage than I think I have. Every single day, I do something that I am afraid to do, that I know I should do. As a result, I become more and more courageous and fearless every single day!"*

Here's mine to help you get started:

I am Jarrod Uddin. I have a name that no one pronounces correctly but I love what my name represents! **I believe in** telling the truth, even when it hurts. **I believe in** facing issues rather than running from them. I used to hate how my voice sounded but I love that I get paid to talk!

I love giving people gifts, making people laugh, cooking, eating, painting and screaming at the top of my lungs while riding insanely fast roller coasters with my closest friends. **I believe** that I am never too young or too old to do ANYTHING! **I love** all of my family, have carefully selected my friends and would 'go to war' for any one of them.

I commit myself daily to doing the things that I know I should do, even if I am afraid. Every time I commit to doing something, all of the right resources show up to help me get it done. **I commit** to learning from my mistakes rather than being trapped by them.

I am great at desk jobs, but they bore me to tears! **I am not the best** at science but am great at English. I get the most joy from helping people overcome their problems and get excited about their individual potentials and futures. **I believe that everyone is supposed to** love their life and do what they are passionate about (every single day). I believe we all have a special part to play in "changing the world", are here for a purpose and must get to work quickly! If anyone is not doing so, **I MUST** motivate them to get going: It's the work that I love **so much** that I would do it for free but am grateful to be getting paid for it! **I do NOT** believe in retirement!

….. I am all of this and more!

Signed: _____

HATERS & FRIENDS YOUR CREW: #SQUAD #RELATIONSHIPGOALS AND THE INEVITABLE *BREAKUP*

Let's start with *Friends.*

The people you hang around matter. As the saying goes, you will become the average of the five people that you spend the most time with. Simply put, if you want to become smarter, hang around those that are smarter than you. If you want to become richer, hang around those with a wealth mentality and the accoutrements to prove it. It may be incredibly uncomfortable, but surround yourself with people who can run circles around you in as many areas of knowledge as possible. People who are exponentially more skilled or hold expertise in a variety of categories. Bottom line, you need people. Whether they be mentors, family or friends. People who will challenge you and make you better. You should never be the smartest person in the room.

The Purpose of Friendships.

The purpose of any relationship is to teach you something. To enhance you, help you heal, or to allow you to develop or grow in some area. Not every friendship is supposed to be life long. And I always try to approach each relationship with this expectation, no matter what kind of relationship it is. With anyone that I associate with, I always ask myself: What is this friendship teaching me? How is it enhancing me? Am I growing? How have I changed? What are they influencing me to do or avoid? Is this friendship supporting me or helping me along the path of my better potential or vision for my life? Answer these questions and then make a good choice about whatever relationship you are in. We typically always have all of the information we need to make a wise choice on whether a relationship is healthy for us, be it romantic or copacetic.

There are relationships that can hold you back from achieving your highest potential. There are relationships that can distract you from building on your greater priorities. There are relationships that can end suddenly and leave you feeling heartbroken and alone. Feeling worthless. Be very careful whom you give your heart to: Efforts spent on pleasing and impressing. Thoughtful gestures, time investments and special commitments are just a few examples of what it means to *give your heart* to someone.

Mile-Deep Friendships.

These are the most valuable kinds of friendships. The ones where you have invested the most time and energy. These are the people who understand your value, and make a return investment of time, energy and commitment. They are the ones that you can call on. The ones that will sharpen you. Call you out on your crap. Make you better.

And you only need a few good friendships like these that are *mile deep.* Beyond the casual surface-level associations. Besides, the demanding pursuit of purpose and the journey to becoming your best, leaves almost no room for people who aren't interested in friendship authenticity. When you understand your worth you will also attract those who will honor it.

And when you find these kinds of rare individuals who are willing to invest their heart in friendship covenant, honor it.

Not every friendship is meant to last.

If you are anything like me, you were probably told as a kid, that the friends you have now, the friendships that you believe will last forever, probably won't be there forever. Of course no one wants to hear that, let alone actually believe it, so we concede to our own dissonance. Until one day, we experience the heartbreak and learn the truth. There are a number of reasons that friendships end. People grow apart and even decide to take different paths in life. Sometimes there is absolutely no intelligent explanation at all. But if someone happens to walk out of your life, after you've made your best friendship investment, it's okay. Let them go. New friendships will come. Healthier friendships. Better friendships.

The Inevitable Breakup:

Ever had a friendship that just ended? Fizzled out? And with no explanation as to why? All of a sudden you just stop hanging out, texting, and the relationship just ends? That happens to everyone. Sometimes it's for a reason and other times it's not. Not everyone will be with you for the long haul of your lifelong journey. And some just don't want to be. That's okay. Let them go. If a friend decides not to be connected to you any longer, then just decide that they have served their purpose and now it's over. Definitely do not be afraid to break up with friends, especially if you find yourself in a position where you are being devalued, disrespected or dishonored.

Some friendships come with a built-in expiration date.

As the saying goes, all good things must come to an end. There is such a thing as a seasonal relationship. Which simply means, there are people will will enter your life for a period of time and then depart when that time is up. People usually enter your life for the purpose of sharing something, helping you grow, or for your learning benefit. They may teach you something you never knew, or bring you some unexpected happiness.

When these kinds of relationships come, it's like a breath of fresh air being breathed into our lives and we usually jump in immediately without evaluating things and believing that it will be a lifelong thing. But when it is time for a seasonal relationship to end, it will usually end suddenly, and oftentimes without an *intelligent* explanation. When seasonal relationships end, they are usually the ones that leave us questioning and often agonizing over why it ended. And the longer we agonize over it, the worse the experience will be.

This has happened to me several times.

I've had several *best friends* like this to enter my life for a period of time and then exit. With no explanation. The relationship can last a month, a year, or even several decades. But when it's over, it's over. and there's nothing else you can do to make the relationship work. Don't worry about the *why*. The reason is not important. The season is over and it is just time to move on. There's nothing *wrong with you.* There's nothing you can do or could have done differently. Let the door close and you'll end up making room for someone new. Someone better. Ultimately, I had to learn to just be grateful for these relationships even though they were short lived. Grateful that someone was willing to take valuable time out of *their* lives to help me, enhance me, and provide something that I may have needed at that moment.

There's nothing more painful than finding out you're disposable...

Especially after you've given of yourself. Your hardest fight and your best of efforts. Whether it was to a person, a job, a project or a relationship. I've had jobs that have ended, friendships that have ended. Things that I thought were supposed to last a lifetime. These are not easy endings to deal with. but when they are over, there's no one to blame. There's nothing to be fixed and nothing you can do to bring it back. It's just time to move on to the next.

Okay... I'll level with you here. You have a ton of value! And to the right person, you will be a dream come true. Priceless! But when seasonal relationships end (friendship, job, etc.) it can easily leave you *feeling* worthless.

I bring this up as a warning because most people will view these relationship endings as a detrimental loss and stay stuck there as a victim. Stuck in the hurt, resentment and disappointment.

They usually allow the hurt to make them question their value and worth, with questions like: what's wrong with me? Why am I not good enough? etc. Don't do that to yourself. Don't make it about you. Understand there is something better right around the corner and that one relationship ending, is essential for making room for the next!

THE TRUTH ABOUT HATERS

Note: If you don't have haters, then you probably aren't achieving enough *wins*. *Wins* will always stir up the envy in others.

A "hater" is someone who wishes that you would have fewer "wins" so that they can feel better about themselves, their laziness and lack of achievement. They are people who will go as far as to sabotage, criticize and tear you down because the agony of watching you succeed, while their dreams are passing them by, is too unbearable. Haters are individuals who see your potential and value through the lenses of their own insecurities. They can see your strengths and wish that they possessed them. The more they focus on you through the eyes of jealousy, the more they begin to resent their own uniqueness.

They may poke fun at you or spread rumors about you to try and bring you down, resenting the fact that you have divine qualities that they feel should be *theirs*. Simply put, haters are people who don't know who they are yet. People always know when they have encountered a "winner"! When someone wishes that they were more popular, confident or smarter, they can't help but to notice how popular, confident and smart YOU are. Even if you don't see it within yourself. They initially begin to feel bad about their strengths, believing the little lies in their head that tell them *your* life is better than *theirs*.

The truth about haters, is they are insecure. They are in pain and hiding it. You have something that they want or else they wouldn't be hating on *you*. The funny thing about a hater is they must wait until YOU achieve a win or make a move before they can plan their next attack, to hate on something that you accomplished. So understand that it is really *you* that has all the power!

The *"Rich Kids"*

I usually don't catch television talk-shows, but I happened to flip past one recently and was immediately drawn in by what happened. On the stage sat five young individuals who apparently were the starring cast of a controversial reality TV show that focused on the lives of these twenty-something millionaires and billionaires showcasing their wealthy lifestyles. What grabbed my attention was an audience member who stood up, took the microphone and verbally attacked these young people for bragging on TV about their wealth. Making the argument that all of the thousands of dollars that they were spending on clothing and fun, was from their parents' bank accounts. Pointing out that the money they were splurging was wealth that they had not earned. The audience member went on and on to say how they should get off of TV because they thought it was a waste of programming and that the tens of thousands of dollars that they were spending on clothing could just as well go towards the "needy".

My thoughts on this….

The lady in the audience is a "hater".

Right in front of her very eyes, were five young people, who had what she believed to be a much better life than hers. Right then it dawned on me. As she was blaming them for having wealth, she was actually revealing the very thing she herself wished that she possessed: (Money, freedom, happiness and an all-around "better life"). At times, it may feel easier to attack the very people that have the stuff that we want, out of sheer jealousy. It's in our nature. She was only attacking a "better life" because a "better life" is what she wanted. Someone else having it and being vocal about it only stirred up her anger and envy. Otherwise, someone else having it should have done her no harm.

When someone chooses to "hate" on you (revealing envy, distaste or harsh verbal criticisms for your achievements or possessions), please understand that it is only because YOU have what THEY want. It's not because you are a horrible person. Conversely, we all have the potential to become the hater ourselves, in that there is always someone else who will have something that we want. The choice to become a hater is on you.

My advice

Don't "hate" on someone because they possess what you think you want. When you do this, you actually prevent the *things* you are hating on from entering into your life. Consider, that the very person that you choose to hate on, could very well be the person you might need to later have as a friend.

So let's practice this. When someone has something you want and you feel the little "green eyed" hater awaking within, before you morph into The Hulk, try this little remedy concoction to tame the hater within:

First, <u>be honest with yourself</u> by admitting within, that what the other person has, is something you really desire to have as well, whatever it may be. Note: There is plenty of delightful goodness in this world for us all to enjoy. Please don't get caught believing the little lie that there is only enough happiness for a few "lucky" people. Believing that lie will make you crazy. It'll make you depressed, thinking that your life is "over" every time you don't get something you want. When you think like this, believing that what someone else has should rightfully be yours, at least one of three more lies will try and enter your mind:

Lie 1: *There is <u>nothing else</u> out there for me (My life is over).*

Lie 2: *There must be something <u>wrong</u> with me.*

Lie 3: *I must find a way to knock them down a few notches (**note:** this one is full-on Hater... like foaming at the mouth!)*

These are all lies. So instead of pondering how you can knock the winner off of their pedestal, instead ponder on the actions and efforts you can begin to take that will ultimately cause those same kinds of wins to come into your life. Maybe you can practice more, study more, be more disciplined, go to try-outs, train harder in the off-season or just commit to doing that thing that you're afraid to do or have been procrastinating on. There is always SOMETHING that you can do to start getting what it is that you really want. When you consider this, you shift from being a victim to someone who accepts control over their situation.

1. **Appreciate** and accept that what someone else has is valuable and that person either made the effort and put in the work to earn what they have or are at the very least an example that winning is indeed possible for you as well.

2. **Celebrate** them for what they have or what they accomplished! There is nothing more refreshing for a winner than to hear someone say they did a great job or a nice congratulations from someone with a genuine heart. This may seem difficult, but if you can muster up the strength to do this, a few awesome things will happen: A) You will actually feel good about yourself. B) You will set yourself apart from all of the other *haters* and you may just make a new friend in the process!

3. **Befriend** other winners. It makes winning so much easier! Birds of a feather indeed flock together. They also think alike, do alike and produce similar results. In this case, wins! When you befriend other winners, sometimes they will share their winning strategies and help you to succeed as well. **Note:**

There is nothing more that a person (who is well aware of their strengths) loves to do, than to help someone else to do something that they themselves are best at. Be kind, be humble and just ask for their help. You may be surprised.

Note: At ALL costs, fight to NOT be the critic!

The difference between haters and enemies:

Haters are jealous and envious individuals who need only switch their focus from "you" to themselves. An enemy, however, is someone who is deeply depressed, and has given up on all hope that they can have any form of a great future. They have bought into the lie that someone else's life is better than theirs and that the best way to gain some relief is to do something about it. They have taken their "hater-ism" to the next level and have made it their mission to take down the one or more person(s) who have what they want. "Hater-ism" is general, but "enemy" is specific and directed towards a specific person or group of people.

One enemy in particular

When I was in college, popularity and social status meant everything to everyone. My school was considered a smaller university, and although there were more than 18-thousand students, it felt like a gigantic high school. It seemed like everyone knew one another. While there, there was a young lady (let's call her Kim), who was the epitome of a hater gone crazy. Each week, on Thursday's, in our student union (where everyone hung out), the floors would be flooded with white sheets of paper at lunch time. Kim had committed herself to writing a weekly gossip article about all of the popular or well-known people at school and would write mostly embarrassing, humiliating and hateful comments about them.

Other times she would spy on people, catching them doing embarrassing things in their personal time, photograph it and print it for everyone to see the following week. She even recruited several lesser known haters to do a lot of the footwork for her. A lot of people's feelings were hurt every week at the hateful and embarrassing things that were being written about them, but because the gossip was so juicy, everyone flocked to the student union each Thursday at noon to grab their copy and read it (especially other haters, for the hope that someone more popular than them would get "knocked down" a few notches. Believing that someone else's demise would make more room for them to rise to the top). Until haters decide to change, they will never achieve what they truly want. Kim never made it inside the "circle" of popularity. She is only remembered for being a supreme hater, and nothing more.

Wisdom: It's really difficult for a hater to effectively unhinge a confident person who loves themselves, flaws and all. If you have weaknesses and flaws in your life, own them. Accept your humanity for what it is. Be okay with it and then tear down the walls you are hiding it behind. Haters love to throw grenades at your walls in efforts to expose what you're hiding. Remove their ammunition.

Note: A critic can only come alive when someone has what they crave. If they would only focus on identifying and building their strengths then they would no longer have this hater complex. They would consequently only have enough time to focus on themselves instead of everyone else.

Not every critic is a "Hater"

Anytime you have committed to a winning track in life (a success trajectory), others will come along with some great ideas on how to make you shine, improve and get better at what it is that you do well.

Sometimes, this coaching and sharpening can be uncomfortable and require us to push beyond limits that are personally inconvenient. When this happens, don't fight the *investor* or the process, and certainly don't label this person a critic or hater. It is often in our human nature to fight personal improvement because we are defending the things that we don't want to fix or improve on.

Note: When you begin to focus on your strengths and start achieving, there will be haters, friends, celebrators, critics, enemies, helpers and teachers that will all appear. Embrace the inevitable.

Note: Your achievement will reveal who other people around you really are or which of the following they will choose to become. Are they a celebrator (or cheerleader, supporting your progress), a critic/hater, friend, enemy or helper? People who have 'unfollowed the crowd' only play the following positions: Friend, Achiever, Celebrator and Helper.

Mastery Level Strategy: *A shot to the heart.*

Find the critics and haters, and kill them with some kindness. Begin by speaking to them at random in the hallway with a smile (this will completely dismantle their game and thrown them off). Shower them with compassion. Share with them something that you admire about them. It's incredibly difficult to hate someone who is showing you compassion and kindness. Ultimately, all a hater really wants is to be "close" to greatness (yes <u>YOU</u>, in their eyes, are greatness). And when you offer yourself up as someone who is touchable, approachable and kind towards *them,* you will reverse their game and slowly turn a hater into a potential ally.

Friends that leave you

Unfortunately, even the best of friends sometimes find themselves unable to stick-around when you seem to be achieving wins, especially if *they* are not. There will be times when you (or they) will get stuff, achieve stuff or win stuff that they may want as well, but are unwilling to push themselves to earn. Because "misery" can't stand to lose its company, they may at times show resentment for the friend that achieved something outside of the norm. Maybe you decided that you needed to work harder, take your life more seriously, not procrastinate or get into trouble, (possible things that you and your friend were accustomed to doing together). They may even accuse you for having "changed". Well here's the stone cold truth of the matter: You HAVE changed, and so should they. You should always be striving to do better, be better, think better, want better, win and live better. All of this requires change and somewhere in there, YOU decided to grow up while they decided to stay put, where it felt safe. That is on them, not you.

KNOW WHEN TO FIGHT AND HOW TO FIGHT

Take a lesson from Reality TV

Reality TV has successfully taught us exactly how to be critics, bullies, haters and enemies, but not how to be REAL friends. The games *they* play are in efforts to compete, overshadow, outshine or outperform their cast mates in an often subtle attempt to knock the other person off of their "throne" (all while being seduced into the "pie mentality" notion that there is only *one* spot at the top). They have taught us that in order to get what you want: (respect, money, love, advancement, elevation), that you must *fight*.

How exactly did you <u>win</u>?

Of course, there is such a thing as healthy competition, however, reality television has turned healthy competition into a vicious battle of who can tear down the other person first (be it with words or fists), and to continue clawing. It may even seem that those who claw the hardest, get the most media attention and are rewarded by society for being vicious within the rings of our pop culture (try acting like this on your job, at school or toward your parents, and it will most likely land you a one-way ticket to suspension, being fired, prison or worse). This is *not* how you *win* in life! I would rather leave a legacy of integrity, compassion, love and high moral character rather than tearing other people down for a few ratings and a momentary spotlight. That is not a win! That's setting yourself up to live a future of shame and loss.

The smartest way to fight back

People who have 'unfollowed the crowd' understand that the best way to fight back is with *wins*, positive victories, self-improvement and completed goals! You should be <u>so busy</u> working on your goals, dreams, and projects and planned victories that you don't even have the time to worry about what a hater might do! You should be so busy at work in fact, that every one of your haters should be on pins and needles, afraid that *you* are about to make your next move, and win!

A haters' whole objective is to throw <u>you</u> off of your game, steel your <u>focus</u> and trick you into not winning anymore. As long as you are wasting your energy entertaining their criticisms, they will be laughing. Haters understand that the more they can get you to focus on them, the less time you will be spending on winning and achieving. At all costs, fight to keep a haters' shenanigans out of your brain space!

Take the battle OFF - line

Recently, I was listening to a popular New York radio show where the host was interviewing a young and upcoming music artist. She had just won several awards for her album and was quickly increasing in popularity. The host asked her to comment on some of her favorite artists, but then asked her to comment on a Twitter feud that she had recently engaged in with another female artist in her category. In explaining the situation, she took more than fifteen-minutes to criticize, berate, name call and hate on the other artist in question.

Note: In life, when you are given a platform and opportunity to respond, fight back or put it to rest, use that platform and opportunity to put out the fire rather than adding fuel to the flames. Pop culture often teaches that any publicity good publicity and that crushing the other person is the best way to win your battles. That strategy is less than smart! Ultimately they over inflate it for media attention and sales, but it is the wrong thing to be known for. All publicity is not "good" publicity, especially if you have to apply for college, scholarships, or a job at some point. When you fire back at someone on social media or engage in a battle online, it only reveals your insecurity.

Consider this:

What IF: You go to a job interview and are asked the question (that most employers will always ask): *"So how do you deal with conflict?"* What would you say? What then if they pull out a tablet that reveals your last twitter *rant* or social media feud? What would you say then? In an employer's eyes, social media is what reveals the actual truth about you. *That's* your <u>real</u> resume. Now of days, rather than asking for your resume, recommendation letters and credentials, most employers request your social handles first before they see anything else. Your paper resume is just the edited highlights of your life but what really matters is your social media content because that is what speaks to how you really handle everyday life.

Note: All social media feuds are a waste of time and the worst way to win a battle. When harsh words are exchanged through social media, one's immaturity becomes etched in online history for the entire world to witness. It's your life's billboard (the place that scholarship committees, schools and potential employers will go to and research to find out more about you). Feuding on social media is indeed where people shoot themselves in the foot.

People who 'unfollow the crowd' understand their <u>enemies</u>:

DISCLAIMER: Just because you have a few people in your life who don't like you, or that "hate on you", doesn't always mean that they are your enemy. Conversely, every friend that offers tough advice or a bit of criticism isn't necessarily a hater, or envious of you. "Enemy" is too heavy a title to use on others, just because you don't get along or have a disagreement. In the 7th and 8th grade I had two bullies named Alex and Damien. They were bigger than me, they taunted me and would constantly try and provoke me to fight them.

When we got into high school, however, we ended up being on the same sports teams where we had to train together, help one another out and work together. Through team sport, we came to learn, value, rely on, trust, and appreciate more about one another than we ever would have known. By the time we became seniors we were all great friends and we still stay in touch. The "bully & victim" relationship we once had was the result of a huge misunderstanding. It was easier to dislike one another and be a bully or victim because we did not know or understand each other.

Question: How well do you know your enemies?

"In the moment when I truly understand my enemy, understand him well enough to defeat him, then in that very moment I also love him. I think it's impossible to really understand somebody, what they want, what they believe, and not love them the way they love themselves. - Ender Wiggin (Enders Game, 2013)

Note: It's almost impossible to bully, despise or hate on someone when you truly know and understand one another.

Note: It takes too much energy to hate. It drains you of the very life force within you. Usually we hate because *they* have poked at, revealed or exposed something inside of us that we hate about ourselves! It's impossible to hate someone without first taking a look in the mirror at our own soul.

ENDING HATE: The next time you find yourself feeling like you hate someone, do this: Take out a sheet of paper. Write out the person's name, what they did to hurt, embarrass or offend you. Then I want you to rate your level of intensity, dislike or anger towards them on a scale from 1 to 10 ("1" feeling mildly offended and "10" feeling downright *broken* inside). How many times this has happened or how many times you have allowed it? (Write that down). Now look introspectively: *Why* did their actions or what they said effect you? (Write that down). Is it possible that they stepped on a deep unhealed wound within you that they were unaware of? Did they knowingly or unknowingly poke at a *weakness* that you've been hiding and have yet to deal with?

Note: If the person who committed the offense was someone like your best friend, someone who understands your weaknesses and knowingly betrayed your trust regardless, then forgive them anyway. Understand, however, that they are not someone that you will be trusting again with confidential information. Again, forgiveness doesn't mean that the offense didn't affect you. It simply means you will not hold on to the hurt or let it poison you. It means that you are committing to learning from the occasion and are moving on. It means that you are releasing the offender from the obligation of having to pay for what they did to you.

Now, what would you really like for that relationship to be like? Would you like for them to treat you well? Would you like to actually be friends with that person? Would you like for them to appreciate you, respect you, and treat you like a friend? Then it's time to have a <u>conversation</u>! (read on)

THE BEST REVENGE

BAD Advice: A very famous television personality recently said: *"When someone does something bad to you, the best revenge is to treat them like they don't exist."*

Warning: This is all wrong! The <u>best</u> revenge is <u>love</u>. Let me explain:

All of us have been or will be disappointed by a friend, family member or someone close to us. It's inevitable. When this happens, at all costs, refuse to harbor anger and resentment. Those emotions don't hurt the other person. They only hurt you. Unfortunately, many of us are taught that our resentment and unforgiveness is our best chance at revenge and power. But it's actually a self-inflicted poison. So often we choose to hold that person in contempt without even having a discussion about the offense, why it happened or seek to understand one another.

People who 'unfollow the crowd' aren't afraid to have the *tough conversations*

If you are someone who has been choosing to sit in anger and unforgiveness, just imagine the amount of success you could you be having right now if your energies weren't focused on feelings of hurt, because of what someone else said to you or did to hurt you. When you allow this to go on without having a healthy conversation, you will have effectively turned a <u>friend into a thief</u> by allowing what they did to you to affect you, and they usually don't even know it. This is called robbing yourself. Have you been robbed?

How to have a *tough* conversation with a friend

A tough conversation is simply a conversation that you don't want to have, but you know that it is necessary. Please understand that when a friend commits an offense against you, they won't always realize the extent that it hurt or affected you. Do them the justice by bringing it to their attention, politely! Plan it out: Know what it is that you want to gain from the talk (Understanding, clarity or maybe there are feelings that need to be expressed). Understand also, that the conversation is only seems tough because this is a relationship that is important to you and you may just be in fear for how what you need to share will be received by the other person.

SECRET TACTIC: When you have to have a tough conversation with someone, whether it is a friend or adult, begin by sitting down next to one another (side-by-side) rather than face-to-face. Psychology tells us that we are naturally more defensive when we are facing people, for this reason: A *problem* is something you *face*. Sitting or standing face-to-face will naturally make one more confrontational and guarded. The psychology behind sitting next to a person says: We are *together,* solving a problem. I always advise the teachers and parents that I train to do this: When you need to have a tough conversation with your spouse or kids, make sure you are sitting side-by-side, rather than face-to-face. The conversation will go much smoother!

Do it in an environment that's peaceful and at a time when you are calm rather than upset. Understand, that a friend or a family member that offended you, more than likely did not intend to hurt, harm or dishonor you. Be prepared to understand *their* point of view also. It is very possible that whatever was done to you or by extension of their actions, they may not even remember the offense! If that's the case, then consider it a good thing! This means you now have an opportunity to open up and share with them the things that affect you. The things that matter to you and all around how you would like to be treated.

Do NOT do it intervention style (this will save them embarrassment and from feeling like they are being attacked or ganged-up on). If the context of the subject matter is tense, then an audience of 2 or more people will only amplify the pressure of it blowing into a full-blown argument or a potential fight. Keep things calm. The hardest part: If this is truly a serious matter, be brave enough and willing to possibly lose that friend for a while. Sometimes when we have something difficult to tell them, we resort to keeping the truth from them (out of fear) because we may believe that the information will hurt or upset them.

Friendship means you care enough about the other person to tell them the truth and be willing to snatch them from the fire; danger and from stumbling in life. Even if it means you suffer from the brush fire (this is love). It means you care enough to have the difficult conversations (conversations that you don't want to have, but are necessary).

People 'who unfollow the crowd' don't judge every friend on the same "scale"

Every friend is different. Appreciate them for it! One friend may be a great listener. Another may not tolerate much drama. Both can still be great friendships even though the two individuals are not the same. I am the kind of friend who will allow you to vent, but for no more than just a couple of minutes… Personally, all of my friends understand that if you bring a problem to me, I am going to offer you a solution and demand that you commit to some form of resolute action! Rather than listening to your problems and leaving you the same way I found you. I refuse to allow people to sit in frustration, anger or upset. Whatever the issue is, I help you to either find the silver lining in the situation or to do something to change it. But I certainly won't allow you to sit still in the issue and be miserable.

Note: Share your heart. Tell the truth. Be vulnerable. Be compassionate. Take the risk. Be a friend.

WHO ARE YOU WHEN THE BATTLE IS OVER?

Note: Sometimes the lessons we learn from the losses are more important than the lessons we learn from the wins. When you lose, do you turn into a complainer? Do you quit? Do you get angry and challenge leadership or the person that won? In my lifetime I have lost in several competitions. But each of those losses helped prepare me for the REAL wins in my future.

True Story

When I was a freshman in high school, I joined the marching band. The three Drum Majors of the band were the top leaders whom everyone held the utmost respect for. They gave all of the field commands, led drills and were the most respected students in the 200-person organization. From the moment I joined the band, I knew that I wanted to be a Drum Major.

t the end of every year, the Band Director would host four-weeks of after-school special training sessions for those who wanted to participate in Drum Major try-outs. I signed up and endured the four-weeks of exercising, push-ups and calisthenics, leadership training and all of the hard work that was required in the process. I gave my all and knew that I would be one of the three that would ultimately be chosen. Unfortunately, I was denied… after giving it my best!

I kept a good attitude nonetheless, stayed in the band and tried out again during my sophomore year. I committed to being a better marcher, a better instrumentalist, respectful and always ready and willing to contribute. I even helped during band fundraisers and remained an all-around team member. When the time came around again for try-outs during my sophomore year, I gave it my very best shot! I was stronger, more efficient and had perfect scores in every area of testing. I was denied… Again.

It was now my junior year. By now, I was one of the most committed members of the band organization. I was always the first one to practices, one of the best instrumentalists in the group, I never complained and I always showed respect toward leadership. Now in my third year, I tried out again for Drum Major, with equal passion, energy and enthusiasm. This time, I was selected!

It felt good when I won because I had fought for it! Not once did I get angry, complain or show contempt for the leaders that had been chosen in the previous years. That summer, before my senior year began, me and my Drum Major partner both spent four intense days of training at Michigan State University's statewide drum major camp, where hundreds of high school Drum Majors from around the state would come for marching, directing and leadership training.

The coaches there were tough on all of us! We were made to memorize music, drill routines on the field, perform special marching sequences and display absolute mastery in every area that we were training for. We were graded on everything from our timeliness, execution, teamwork and <u>attitude</u>!

At the end of the four day period, the Band Director from Michigan State University awarded <u>me</u> and one other person with the Big Ten Award, which meant we received the highest scores out of the entire camp of leaders. To this day, that award remains the highest honor given to high school drum majors in the state of Michigan.

Note: Each year that I lost out on the Drum Major try-outs, I learned something valuable that would help me for the following year. There will be times where <u>you</u> are perfect for the role, but they just need to see how badly you actually want it. In some cases, the REAL competition is after the battle is over: Your ability to keep a good attitude after a rejection is far more important than bringing your A-game to the challenge.

Note: The losses and oppositions are there so that <u>you can prove</u> how badly you really want it, and to keep *out* the <u>other people</u> who *don't* want it as badly as you do.

Those who don't want it that badly, don't deserve it, but those who are willing to fight for it, do! Not once did I ever complain. I didn't sulk. I didn't throw a tantrum, break something or put my fist through a wall and most importantly: **<u>I did not quit the team</u>**. I hung in there, congratulated those who did win and I continued to show up with my support to help the team to keep winning. Those virtues allowed me build strength, leadership and morals that helped me secure several victories following.

Story continued...

The day that I won the Big Ten award at Drum Major camp, my mom was there to congratulate me, and even congratulated my Drum Major partner, Damien, for having won Drum Major at our school. (Remember Damien? He was one of my 7th grade bullies turned "friend"). As I was walking to the car to go home, after what had been an exhausting weekend, there was this one kid who ran up to me to try and challenge my scores. He was obviously upset that he didn't win the award and was willing to protest. Needless to say, no one paid him any attention. Don't let the hater be <u>you</u>.

Note: There is a difference between competition and competitive jealousy. Jealous people never think that they are in fact jealous.

My definition of **jealousy**: Being sick because someone else received something that you wanted. My advice: Congratulate the winner, go home, get better and try again next time. Never challenge the winner. Just train harder!

Note: People who 'unfollow the crowd' fail <u>all the time</u>... But they never quit until they win.

Do you really have to be your BEST?

No, but you should. Would you be okay if I told you, that your BEST probably was not good enough? Would you be okay if your best was better than everyone else's, but what was needed at the time, was someone *else*? Are you willing to explore the possibility that the level to which you apply yourself may need to increase or upgrade? Usually, our best just isn't good enough. That means you need a new "best". When you did not win or earn something you wanted, the first time around, use that as your chance to grow into a better *you.*

Never get stuck into thinking that your minimum or even best efforts should be immediately accepted or rewarded. Have you ever had a teacher that handed you your homework back and said: *"Sorry…. But this isn't good enough. Go back and do it again"?* And then you have to go back, tweak it and fix it several times until it's nearly flawless? I would rather someone require me to be the best *me* possible by making me do the work, rather than allowing me to go out into the world and failing because I am unprepared.

The right way to fail

Plan to win. Meditate on how you can win. Strategize it. Try it. If it doesn't work the first time, then it's not a real fail as long as you try it again. This time re-examine your former strategy. Remove from your plan what didn't work last time or simply change it. Ask questions. Get some help. Make it better. Try it again (Wash and repeat). *Average* people quit after the first *fail* and lack the courage to endure the lessons and the growth. Do not let this be you.

You need to fail!

You need to have some failures in your life. If you have not competed in anything or have never taken on a goal that was bigger than you because you were afraid of failing, then you have been robbing yourself of the best life lessons you could have ever learned. The failures are what help you to become resilient, strong and grow into one of the wisest <u>teachers of *life*</u> that anyone can sit under. If you want to succeed in life then <u>fail faster</u>!

"I won't even work with you unless you have failed at least one-hundred times!"
- Daymond John (*Shark Tank, ABC*)

Personally, I've failed so many times in my life that I'm not afraid of the pain, correction, embarrassment, money lost, energy spent or of trying something one-hundred times until I get it right. Failures are the best training ground you will ever practice on and will prepare you to win in life when the real competition shows up! You will <u>always</u> win if you don't quit!

You will not fail if you have <u>focus</u>:

FOCUS: Saying "no" to everything that gets in the way of you finishing your goal. As soon as you commit yourself to achieving something, everything else will be fighting for your attention: There will be a party. Friends will want you to come hang out. There will be a TV show that you just *can't* miss. There will always be <u>something</u> fighting for your focus. Do not be afraid to say "no" to these distractions. Dedicate yourself to your wins. It will be worth it! Before you dive-into focus, plan a special reward for yourself that you will have as soon as the goal has been achieved and the *win* has been secured. This will help keep you motivated and focused for your achievement.

Note: Even while you are focusing on your goals, you still have to obey your parents, do your homework, chores, and your part-time job if you have one, etc. Those are virtues, responsibilities and values, <u>not</u> distractions. So the rule here is: ***You cannot sacrifice one principle for the other...*** in other words, if you feel like homework or chores are getting in the way of you focusing on your goal, too bad. You still have to do them, and use your <u>personal free time</u> to work on your goals.

Homework:

Step 1:

First, think of a goal. Something that you really want and can begin to take action on over the next seven days. It could be landing a particular job, running for an office at your school, scoring a certain number of touchdowns or making the fastest time during the 100-yard dash at a meet (if you're an athlete). Whatever that goal is, think of it and write it down. Then, I want you to identify with the true and honest sentiment behind why you want to achieve this goal. Identify your *why,* and it must be strong. What will obtaining that goal actually do for you? How will it make you feel? How <u>exactly</u> will achieving this goal change your life? Lastly, what will you reward yourself with once you have achieved this goal? Write those things down.

Step 2:

Find a friend that you trust! One that will cheer you on to your finish. Share your goal with them, your daily action plans and then ask them to hold you accountable for getting them done. Something a friend and I do quite often, is we will both write a personal check for $100 to a random charity that we would really prefer not to support (and place it inside an addressed envelope with a postage stamp). We will then give one another our envelopes. If by the end of the week, our goals are not completed (with evidence of completion), the other person will drop that envelope in the mail and the person will have to kiss $100 goodbye! You do not have to do anything as drastic, but try it with a ten dollar bill or something of value.

Step 3:

Take a massive leap toward this goal with deliberate action. Don't stop until it is achieved!

THE PARENT
ISSUE

I remember the very first time I tried to rent a car on my own. I was a twenty-year old college student on my way to hang out with my other college friends for the weekend in Atlanta. In order to make the three-hour drive, I needed to rent a dependable vehicle. I had always been a responsible driver, had never gotten a speeding ticket and was accident free. I had met all of the requirements to prove that I was a responsible young adult and worthy of renting a car, or so I thought.

As I walked up to the counter to fill out the car rental forms and pick up the vehicle, the first thing the attendant said was: *"Thank you sir. Are you at least 25-years of age or older"?* I was not, of course, and because I did not understand the rental policies, I went on to talk about how I had my own car insurance, a clean driving record and more than enough money to pay for the rental, to which she retorted: *"I understand all of that sir but unfortunately we are unable to rent to anyone that doesn't meet the minimum age requirement".*

So there is some very solid brain research and several statistics revealing that people under 25-years of age do not have brains that are fully developed yet. Scientists have concluded that the frontal cortex, the area of the brain that controls reasoning and helps us think before we act, isn't fully developed until we are at least 25-years of age. This part of the brain is still changing and maturing well into adulthood.

So basically, the part of the brain that helps us assess and respond to danger, take fewer risks and make wiser choices, is underdeveloped and still "cooking", hence they believe that we young people are *"act* first, *think* later", and unable to be trusted with something as important as a borrowed vehicle. As I dug deeper into my research, this belief, I found was further substantiated by the number of car accidents involving teens, which is why rental companies are hesitant to rent cars to people under 25 (and those that do, charge almost double in fees!).

They say that we risk our lives doing "stupid" stuff. Things like:

The Fire Challenge

The "fire challenge" is an activity where someone takes off their shirt, douses their bare chest with a flammable liquid (lighter fluid, gasoline or alcohol) and then sets themselves on fire while being video recorded and later posted online for views and "likes".

So psychologically, the challenge is to see how close one can come to death, while also putting out the fire quickly enough without actually dying or being burned. This is thrill seeking on a highly dangerous and life threatening level.

The Cinnamon Challenge

The objective of this challenge is to film oneself swallowing a spoonful of ground cinnamon in under 60-seconds without drinking anything, then posting the video online. The challenge is difficult and carries substantial health risks because the cinnamon coats and dries the mouth and throat, resulting in coughing, gagging, vomiting and is the cause of many premature deaths. Other side effects are throat irritation, breathing difficulties, and risk of pneumonia or a collapsed lung.

The Knockout Game

The "knockout game" is unique in the fact that it harms unsuspecting victims of any age, gender or race. (Closely related to a hate crime) One or more people attempt to knock-out an unsuspecting victim, often with a single sucker punch (at any place and at any time), all for the amusement of the "attackers" and their friends. In some cases the attacker has been charged with a hate crime, but argued that they were only doing it for the fun of it.

And there are many more…

Drinking and "other substances" of choice

Let's take a lesson from King Solomon. He goes down in history for being the wealthiest man who ever lived and is also known for being one of the wisest. On today's standards he would be worth about $222-Trillion! Out of his wisdom he said that alcohol and "strong drink" is not for those wanting to be <u>kings</u> (rulers, owners, wealthy, respected and prosperous). In his own words, he is famous for saying: "*Alcohol* (strong drink) ***is for those who are ready to die!***"

Question: Is that you? Are you really ready to die?

Simply put: If you understand who you are, value your life, purpose and future, then drinking and partaking in "substances" <u>is not for you.</u>

Simply put, drinking and engaging in "substances" is what people <u>do</u> in order to escape reality, period. **Question:** Is your reality that depressing where you feel the need to escape from it? (Seriously, if it is, then make sure you do ALL of the homework I prescribed).

Those who say they like to drink or use substances "for fun" or to "have a good time" are either in denial or foolish. They do not know who they *are* yet. Nothing good ever came from substance abuse: (fighting, DUI's, driver's licenses being suspended, drunk driving accidents, alcohol poisoning, painful addictions, stealing, premature deaths… stuff like that). There are some who argue that drinking or smoking an illegal substance makes them more intelligent. The truth is, these are mind altering substances that cause subtle to increasing hallucinations, making you believe in realities that aren't even real.

The CRAZY part is that when the party's over and they wake up to a two-day hangover, all of the problems that they were drinking in order to escape are <u>still there</u>!

Note: People who 'unfollow the crowd' are not drawn in, fooled by, nor do they risk their very lives on cheap thrills. A solid sense belonging and clarity of purpose is the greatest visceral rush you will ever experience. When you have worked to develop your strengths, find your path and have achieved some *wins,* you will not be careless with your life. You will fight to protect it.

It's not just young people that are doing these things. People of all ages engage in careless behaviors. People only act this way because they don't yet know who they are yet (even if they are fifty-years old)! When you don't know who you are, you become careless with your life. Once you do understand who you are and what you should be doing with your life, you start to value it more. It *then* becomes something worth protecting.

The fault in our parents

Because of the increase in popularity of these dangerous activities, our parents often believe that we lack the wisdom to make good choices, so they concede to believing that they must make our choices <u>for us,</u> or at the very least give us the *third-degree* when we don't make the right ones. They sometimes forget to mention that they were once our age and were sometimes even more thoughtless if they are open to admitting so. Here's why they come down on you so hard. Oftentimes adults have made mistakes and choices that they believe (have or could have) "ruined" their lives. Choices that they regret. And when they see someone else showing *signs* of making the same mistakes they did, they are reminded of that once old "choice", embarrassment or screw-up that they themselves once made.

So rather than turning those into peaceful teaching moments, where they gently share *their* mistakes, screw-up's and lessons learned, they often choose (out of protective fear) to attack the *person* who might be showing signs of walking down that same path (you). My challenge to the parents and previous generations reading this, be willing to get humble and share the very benefit of your mistakes and screw-up's that *you* had in life. Ultimately, the generation you spawned, will learn more from those stories than they will a punishment or lecture. I teach K-12 teachers to govern their classrooms with love, compassion, understanding and patience; Not by "bringing down the hammer". Most often, all of us, are just one shared lesson away from a positive turn-around.

Ancient Proverb: *Diligent hands <u>will rule</u>, but laziness ends in <u>forced</u> labor.*

BEFORE YOU GRADUATE COLLEGE, KNOW THIS.

Note: If you don't have a plan, then plan on failing… painfully.

The "Land of Paradise" and the "ditch" below

We all have dreams. We all have potential. We all have a place that is set for us to arrive at in life where our passions, skills and strengths will make work feel like a pleasure. A place where we are celebrated for our individuality, rewarded for what we do best and creatively impact the world around us. I call this place the "Land of Paradise". It is a very real place. One where our purpose and dreams come to life. It is real and <u>you</u> are supposed to be there.

Like so many of my friends, I grew up believing that if I could just make it to college, that my future in this glorious "Land of Paradise" would be secured and certain. We often buy into the myth that if we can manage to survive all four-years of undergrad that life will hand us a golden entry pass into the coveted dream life that we desire, right on the other side of graduation. Unfortunately, that is not how it works.

(Take a look at the illustration)

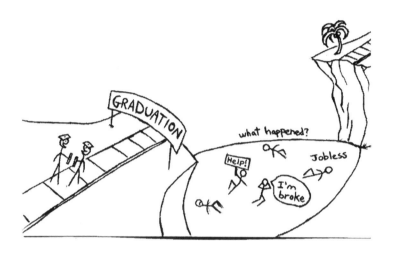

The Truth

Above is my little illustration of the road to graduation. Most people make college *graduation* their entire goal and neglect to plan for anything else beyond that! They put in a ton of work during their senior year, do well on their exams, pass, walk across the stage at graduation where they shake the hand of the school President and are handed a shiny piece of paper that might as well say: *"Congratulations! You've got potential!"*

They stand there waiting around for the golden doors of opportunity to open, but while they are waiting, they fall off the proverbial cliff that they did not see coming, and land in the "ditch", the place that I call "average".

Note: Life comes at you fast!

THE BIG LIE:

The world owes me something because I graduated college.

THE BIG TRUTH:

The world owes us NOTHING but air to breathe. That's it. Beyond that, you must use that fighting chance to live and thrive. It is up to <u>you</u> to do everything with that chance as you possibly can.

You *must* have a plan!

A huge problem with our generation is that we are mostly waiting for big opportunities to fall into our laps without actually going out there and doing the work that our passions require. A successful life demands that we work our talents to see them evolve into something amazing over a period of time, through consistency, diligence and determination, sacrifice and some occasional criticisms and upsets. The "cliff" (in the illustration) is just a little pain so that we can choose who we will *become* after the *fall*.

If you don't have a vision or at the very least, a plan for what you will do upon graduation, then plan on failing! Plan on delaying your arrival to the peak of your greatest potential. Plan on working a job that you hate. Where someone else will *tell* you who you are because you didn't do the work to discover it for yourself. Making a plan is the most important thing for you to be doing right now. The great thing about a vision is it has the motivational powers to pull you forward and upward, out of the "ditch" and into the "Land of Paradise".

A Vision, must be clear, potent, thrilling, and a bit scary. A vision is not what someone *told* you that you should be doing with your life. It's all about how the best version of you is serving humanity with your strengths, passions and talents. The stuff that makes you come alive. Besides, you only have enough time, space, energy, and bandwidth to live <u>one</u> life. Yours. Not someone else's expectation of you.

Note: Potential means absolutely nothing without a solid plan.

Lie: Following your passion is a waste of time.

Truth: It's only a waste of time if you're sitting back waiting on the moon and the stars to drop into your lap. You must take action!

Most college graduates who do not secure a plan for their futures, fall over the "cliff" and land right in the "ditch". Eventually they find some sort of a job and take it because they are broke and need the money and over time they settle into an average existence.

In the land of "average", people wake up in the morning and punch the alarm clock at the same time, every day and dread getting up. They haul themselves out of bed to go to a job that they hate but show up because they have to. Because that job wasn't their original dream for themselves and they really don't want to be there, they end up doing just enough not to get fired. They make average money and can't take a break until someone *tells* them they can take a break. They can't take a vacation until someone *tells* them they can take a vacation. At the end of the day, they come home feeling mentally exhausted, but have difficulty believing that they can do anything else because they have now acquired credit card debt, more bills and a lifestyle that they more than likely cannot afford. So they stay stuck in their average situation, go to sleep, and wake up the next morning to do it all over again. **That is no way to live your life.**

Note: The land of "average" is a dangerous place. A dark abyss where anyone who remains there for too long loses his or herself entirely. Staying in the land of "average" is essentially giving up on life.

Maybe this lifestyle doesn't sound all that bad to you. But…

Consider this:

Is comfortable one day working a job that you hate for the rest of your life? Is it comfortable watching others have big wins while you're having none? Is it comfortable watching other people live their dreams, while yours pass you by? Right in your very DNA are dreams and passions that you are supposed to do. Therefore you can do something else, but you will always feel out of place and unfulfilled. There is nothing comfortable about being average.

Okay. I'll level with you.

Maybe your plan is to work a job for a while and one day you're going to have enough money saved to go back to school or invest in your real dream. But the problem with "one day" is that it never really happens! If you have not constructed a clear and potent vision along with a sequence of goals to help you get there, then you can forget about that dream ever happening! Until you have that dream and plan written down on paper and have committed to *making it happen* then it is not real!

As long as your dream is in the future it will never be in your present. The term "one-day" is an excuse for not doing something about it right now, out of fear of disappointment: (*"What if it doesn't work? What if I try and fail a few times? I don't want to <u>feel</u> ashamed, let down, sad or depressed. So I'll just stay where I'm at and get comfortable"*). As a result, you will never actually end up doing anything about it. Your dreams and future are way too important, not to do something about them right now!

Note: Until your dream becomes a *right now* goal, then it is not real! It will not happen until you commit to doing at least one thing about it today!

My second favorite movie scene of all time comes from *The Dark Knight Trilogy.* Just when it seems Batman is trapped on the top floor of a skyscraper in Hong Kong, corned and about to be gunned down. He activates Skyhook: A surface-to-air recovery system that pulls him from the building, through the window and into the air via a harness that was attached to an inflatable balloon, drawn to his plane flying past. Rescuing him from imminent danger.

Note: You can come out of the "ditch" any time you choose, by just taking one action.

SECRET SAUCE: It's not about the shiny credentials and honors that may accompany a college education. It's about how well you can take a "fall", and how long it takes before you stop feeling sorry for yourself. How fast you can get back up! There is nothing better than a person who has taken a "fall", has been made to feel like nothing, and then got back up and proved to themselves that they could "do something".

Added point: There is <u>always</u> something that you can do about your situations! Even when it seems there is no solution, you need only become creative. Here are a few things you can do if you find yourself stuck in the land of "average" after graduation:

Don't be afraid to work an average job.

Just don't stay there long! One of the coolest things about working a job that you hate is that your creative mind will begin to reveal to you the place that you really desire to be. Even if you had never thought of it before. Anytime that you truly feel <u>stuck</u>, your mind switches over to "survival mode". Your brain has the power to creatively strategize various ways of escape. Those are the times when you will receive the best ideas, clarity, goals and a strategy to make it happen. All while working a job that you hate.

YOU MUST CREATE YOUR OWN EDUCATION

You have two educations. The one that's provided for you and the one that you create! The first thought and misconception of people who fall off the "cliff" is that <u>more education</u> is their answer out. So they jump back in school for another degree, acquire more debt and usually end up back in the same situation. They are missing the lesson here. What you need is the education that you didn't get, the one you are to create on your own.

One way you can do this is through reading. Once you decide the dream you want to live, the career you want to have and the legacy you want to build, go do some heavy research. Visit your local bookstore. Find all of the magazines and books that deal with that topic or field and dive-into the reading! Reading expands your mind to possibilities and ideas that you may never have thought possible. It allows you to live someone's life vicariously through the pages. Statistically speaking, if you were to read one book per month (on one particular topic), did you know that you would have enough knowledge to be considered an expert in your town?

Additionally, if you continue the process for three years you could be considered an expert in your state (regarding that topic). If you were to do this for a total of five years you would be considered an expert nationwide. What's more, is authors often leave clues behind in their books. Ideas that may provide the very answer you need to get started. These ideas can help you to launch and arrive at the very place you desire to be.

Note: Did you know that over eighty-percent of college graduates never commit to picking up a book and reading it after graduation?! People who 'unfollow the crowd' never graduate from the virtue of reading, learning or enhancing their minds. Do not neglect the power of reading! Do not be average.

Hunt down an *investor*

Also understand that there is certainly someone out there doing the very thing that you desire to do, and on the level that you want to do it. Find them. Study their success, but more importantly, study their beginnings and their path. Do as much research as you possibly can about them and their industry that you desire to be a part of. Come up with a short list of questions that you would potentially ask them regarding paving your path to their area of success. When the time is right, reach out to them (A handwritten letter via snail mail is best). The guidance that these mentors can offer is sometimes more valuable than the cost of a formal education. Take their input seriously and do the work.

If you are reading this right now, then this is your homework. Get er' done!

Note: Most people are **depressed** because they haven't done what they know they are supposed to do. Doing *just* enough is not enough to succeed. Wanting something and *doing* something are two completely different things.

TAKE A CHANCE ON YOURSELF

I was in the car and on my way to the Detroit Airport. My aunt had managed to hook me up with a job in Washington, D.C. and the bosses there wanted to meet with me. It was a position that I knew could be very lucrative if I took it seriously and applied myself. I had recently graduated college. I was beyond broke and I needed the money but knew that I would be absolutely miserable. It was a desk job and just the thought of resorting to working a job because I "had to" drained me of my energy and motivation. I wanted to turn on the radio and listen to some music to take my mind off of the reality of the situation, but couldn't because someone had broken in my car and took my radio, so I had nothing to listen to, only silence. There's something about silence that has a way of making you "face yourself". Here's what I was facing:

It had been nine months since I had graduated college. I was bouncing from apartment to apartment, sleeping on friends' sofas, and I had yet to find a job. My car was the only thing that I had in my possession in addition to $20 in my wallet. I also had my cell phone, which rang incessantly from debt collectors looking for me to pay them their money on the debt that I had accumulated in college.

I had managed to run up over $13,000 in credit card debt during my junior and senior year in college. Buying "stuff" and having absolutely no way to pay it back. You would think that I would have something to show for it, but the problem is, when you are in a depressed state, money is a neutral force, meaning if you are depressed, then the only things you spend it on are things that keep you in depression. All I knew is that now, I was "stuck" with a huge "mess" to clean up, and had no other choice but to take the job offer in D.C. It was the only offer on the table.

Depression began to set in even further. How in the world did I end up like this? It was right in that moment, right when I thought I was stuck with no way out, that an idea came to me! I remember a cousin of mine urging me to stop by a particular agency in the city that was on the way to the airport. Right then I remembered her saying that they are always looking for people with my skills set to travel, speak and do sales. It was a long shot. I didn't want to be late for my flight, but I knew this could be my last chance. The agency was only two exits away so I decided to get off the freeway and head in.

Once inside, I introduced myself to the receptionist and only requested that she accept and pass my resume along to the relevant parties in case there were any future openings. She immediately responded: "Oh wait, you're actually in luck! Our Vice President and Directors are here right now and I'm sure they would love to meet you if you have a moment." So I stuck around. They escorted me into a conference room where they requested that I stand and read three scripts out loud. Once finished, they asked me to stick around in order to introduce me to a few other Directors at the agency. They were impressed with my interview and impromptu audition and hired me on the spot!

I was there so long that I almost missed my flight to D.C., but I felt <u>alive</u> again! That year, I was paid to travel the entire nation as a Narrator and Public Announcer for the International Auto Show. It was my dream job. I had stumbled on the very place that combined my unique blend of talents, passions and strengths, and would pay me to do something that I loved. I ended up earning enough money to become completely debt free in only a few months and was having a blast living my dream life.

Your Wings Do Work

As you can imagine, there were a few members of my family that were livid with me (excluding my aunt)! They couldn't believe that I would turn down a job like the one offered to me in D.C. I kindly thanked my aunt for all of her efforts and support but ultimately I had to follow my heart and do what legitimately <u>felt right</u>. You will have to do the same in your life. In those moments of fearlessness and courage I felt like I had pulled myself out of the land of "average" and into the land of "paradise". But I was willing to take the risk. I was willing to be wrong. I was willing to try and fail. I was willing to take the risk and possibly be homeless for another 9 months. But I refused to become a "what-if" person. Spending night after night lying awake in bed. Wondering how my life would have been had I chosen to take the risk?

I saw my other friends following the standard "safe job" track but not making much money, not finding any true happiness, real fun or fulfillment. I felt like I knew where that path ended. But electing the riskier option was like walking through a huge door of endless possibilities. Everyone was working a job that they seemingly hated. And all I knew is that if I didn't take this chance that's exactly what my life was going to be like. So I took the chance... What will be your chess-move when the opportunity presents itself?

Note: Choose what's in your heart. Choose what you know is right. And move quickly.

Who is writing on your script? Because the story that you allow anyone else to write for you is going to be a version that pleases them. But at your expense. One that serves their needs, not yours. You have a choice. You can write your own story or you can allow someone else to write it for you. But I promise you this. It will be basic. Without color. It will be their dream. Not yours.

Note: Sometimes you will have to take the risk of upsetting the very people who love you most, in order to save your own life!

Question: When that time arrives, who will you become? A <u>character</u> in someone else's life or the <u>author</u> of your own?

BEFORE YOU RUN OFF TO GRAD SCHOOL, DO THIS FIRST!

My advice to college grads. Before you run off to grad school. First, ask this of yourself: Why exactly am I going to grad school? Is it because your future job requires a Master's degree? Is it because your job prospects look low? Or is it because you just don't know what else to do with your life just yet and grad school seems like a safe option? Many of the college seniors that I mentor initially intimate to me that they've "dipped their toes in the water", taking unpaid internships to try and gain some experience or career prospects upon graduation, only to get cold feet and dash back inside the four walls of higher education, afraid to come back out.

Fact, it's a cold, cruel and scary world out there, and none of us wants to be homeless or jobless. I get it. Which makes jumping back in school a comfortable and familiar option. Careful though. I was at one point in this same boat. About nine months after my college graduation, I stumbled upon the job of a lifetime. But two years after hitting the salary ceiling I wanted more. I knew there was more out there, but I just wasn't sure what or where. So like most opportunity seekers, I went to grad school for a masters in business, believing that more education would equate to more success. Wrong.

I didn't need more education. I needed mentorship and guidance. I needed to figure out my real identity. I needed to develop my talents and strengths and then locate a scene where I could express them and be appreciated for who I was. But instead, I jumped into an accelerated grad school program. Thirteen months and $50,000 later I found myself back in the same position. Still not knowing who I was and without a clue as to my next steps in life (except this time I had another shiny degree and five figures worth of debt).

So if you should be so lucky as to find yourself in such a position, at these bitterly painful crossroads and you are contemplating grad school, do this first:

Create your own education:

1. Finish this book.

2. Choose some sort of career pathway. Preferably something you are truly passionate about. What is it that you want to do with your life? Search for available opportunities and what those opportunities require.

3. Find a mentor. Preferably someone in your field of expertise that has the career you want and is making a living on the level that you would like achieve. Study their accomplishments. Reach out and look for opportunities to be mentored, coached or even interview them on their paths. What were their regrets? Failures? What are their recommendations on formal education and what is required to reach their career status? You may be shocked at their answer. Mentorship and coaching has a special way of fast tracking your learning and makes sure that you stay accountable for achieving results, ahead of the game and ahead of your competition. Beyond this, search online for some success seminars and local live-learning events. Invest the $100 - $1000 that those seminars might require before you flush $20K or more down the drain on more post secondary education that may lead you to nowhere.

4. Select a travel abroad program for six months to a year OR

5. Save all of your spare money and travel somewhere. Take a trip with some friends that you enjoy spending time with. Either fly around the world, or just pick a spot on the map, gas up the car and GO. Even if it is just in the next state over. Traveling opens up a whole new world of perspective. I've taken several spur of the moment road trips to New Orleans,

Nashville, Chicago, South Carolina, and abroad to Central America, all at the spur of the moment. Each time my friends and I have traveled someplace, some amazing things happen. First, we end up having the time of our lives being adventurous, immersing ourselves in new cultures, foods, making new friends and lifetime memories. But there's something else that traveling does. The change of environment has a way of clearing your mind and offering clarity of focus. You begin to see yourself and the world in a whole new light. Creativity begins to flow as you refresh and relax and oftentimes solutions and clarity of purpose come to the forefront of your mind and imagination.

6. Take on a side hustle or a community service project to either learn a new skill or gain experience. Preferably in your special area of interest.

7. Or just take a job. Something oblique, off of the beaten path. You may discover you actually like whatever it is. Best case scenario, you find out that you utterly hate it. This is good. Pain and dissatisfaction has a way of revealing to us where it is we would rather be, which is a great way to unlock your next steps.

DO SOMETHING CRAZY

During my second year out of college, I was on a roll! I was traveling the world, working two of my dream jobs and having the time of my life! But I still wanted more and was open to exploring a new challenging money making opportunity! So I decided to create my own side business hustle as an independent contractor selling vitamins. It was with a network marketing company. The kind where you get to recruit and build your own team with the potential for unlimited income.

It was one of the hardest things I had ever done, but I quickly learned who I was and what I was capable of achieving. I got to be mentored by some amazing business owners. I learned lessons and pushed through, what I believed to be impossible challenges, that are to this day priceless to my growth education. There's no greater teacher than the lessons learned when trying to sell a $500 vitamin box to a stranger off the street. I recruited my 6-person sales team off of the street, trained them, groomed them and earned my first ever 5-figure paycheck at the age of 23. Those lessons I learned back then have made me fearless today, anytime I have to do something that might take more courage than what I think I possess.

Lesson: Do something daring, something you know that will help you grow. Something that takes more courage than you think you have and give it everything you've got. You will quickly find out who you are. This is how you grow. Leap without a clear landing in sight. Do not wait on too much proof before you get started. Don't wait for permission. Don't ask a ton of people their opinion before you take action. Their fear will talk you right out of what could be an insanely phenomenal opportunity to learn, grow and become the person you are supposed to be! Needing constant approval or permission is an indicator that you are not sure of your own ideas or are just operating in fear or even worse, are unsure of your chosen path.

This is crucial if you are ever looking to start a business, create a podcast or launch anything proprietary at all. The kinds of businesses, ideas and individuals that people want to support and follow are those who are confident in their direction and dreams. I cannot emphasize how important this is, especially in sales or when trying to sell a product. If people sense that you need them more than they need your offering, they are almost immediately turned off. People are always attracted to those who are self-motivated and fired up about their ideas and dreams, not to those who are permission seekers. There is of course a time to do market research, but there is also a time to just launch.

A friend of mine was contemplating starting an online comedy show with some friends. The 10-minute show, would air weekly, star a panel of two other friends highlighting the week's current events (both political and pop culture) and would be delivered in a funny and engaging format. Brilliant idea! With the potential to attract thousands, even millions of weekly viewers. But instead of just getting started, he proceeded to ask several other people, every week, their thoughts. If they would watch the show or support the idea. This kind of validation seeking eats away at your available energy and momentum. The longer you wait, the weaker you become.

Immediate action on an idea has a special momentum attached to it that causes success. But the longer you wait, fear sets in and failure to launch becomes inevitable. Fast-forward a year later, he still has not taken one footstep of action on this idea.

This sort of fear based thinking will stall and fail every dream and idea, no matter how deeply it resonates with you heart. Action in spite of fear is critical. When it's in you, you must fight like crazy to achieve and finish. This is what will set you apart. The *crowd* always waits on external validation, permission, ease of motion and a clear landing before they launch. But not you! The best wins you will ever have are the ones you will fight for. The ones where you had to struggle to finish. It will get tough somewhere along the way. That's the test. How badly do you really want it? And you will need to push through to the finish. The *fame* and the negative ego will not be sufficient to sustain you in the success battle. Your *why* has to be stronger than that! It has be connected to something deep in your heart and it must be about advancing other people or else you will burn out.

As the saying goes, *build it and they will come.* So stop waiting for permission, likes and approval and just get started. As said before, all ideas come with an expiration date. Launch, and the buyers will come. Launch, and the viewers will come. Launch, and more ideas will come on how to expand, up level, and create a much larger impact. Be consistent and you will become well known for your creation, impact and young legacy. So often we want the end result of a finished work but are unwilling to leap. Launch first and the rest will take care of itself!

SHOW &
TELL.
THE SMART
RESUME.

Maybe you've acquired an Ivy League pedigree. Maybe you've read 100 books this year. While that's all well and good, nowadays, employers and gatekeepers who hold the keys to the career opportunity you may be seeking, could actually care less about what you know and more about what you can produce.

One of the hardest challenges when coming out of college is proving to an employer that you are worth taking a shot on. Particularly when you don't have the experience that the job warrants. Then again, how are you able to gain experience without a job opportunity that will provide you with said experience? Basically, you need proof that you are who you say you are and that you can effectively produce what you say you can produce! So how do we acquire this glorious proof?

This is where your side hustle comes in. Many times we don't realize that our experiences, side projects and community service efforts, or that side business that you started has supplied you with some extremely valuable skills that can make your resume pop! They help us to discover what value we can produce and give us several reference points that prove to employers that we can get them results.

To this day, the top section of my resume boasts a section called *"Career Highlights"*. This is where I list at least four achievements, wins or successes that I have produced as a result of working one of my side hustles. I list these before my general work experience, even before listing my education. Even though I am currently doing exactly what I love, that resume garners me tons of job offers via email from employers wanting me to come and work for them. Bottom line, the *SMART* resume leverages your strengths and experiences acquired through your side hustle and makes you a stronger contender in the job market.

THE BEST DAY OF YOUR LIFE

The best day of your life is when you see an opportunity to become who you want to be and you take a chance on it. Against everyone who said it wouldn't work. Against all of the so called evidence that said you couldn't do it. But you do it anyway. You put all of your heart, passion and energy on the line and it works! The tough times in your life where you don't know what's going to happen next, when you possibly feel like a failure. When you feel trapped with a dream that no one seems to understand but you. That time in your life where you feel as if you're running a marathon all by yourself. The real test is how much time you waste feeling sorry for yourself after you get knocked down. Get up, fast!

The most frustrating feeling is when you are on your way. Following the plan. When you have decided on a course of action and have made up in your mind that this plan is it and there is no looking back. And all of a sudden that little voice in your head that you can't seem to ignore speaks up. The voice that's reminding you of the dream and potential that you gave up on. You try and ignore it but you know it's still there.

I urge you to listen to that voice. That little inner-conviction that's trying to warn you that something's not right. Find that feeling and pay attention to it. Do something about it. There's only one thing that's more important than your *why*. And it's called *action*. Success never happens while you're standing still. Success and victory always seem to be connected to movement. Not waiting for certainty before you take make a move. Learn to leap, even when there is no clear landing. Either way, success never happens while you are standing still.

Previously, I asked you the following question: *What would you go and do if there was no way that you could fail? What one dream, goal or task would you purse?* But now, I'd like to revise that question to this: *What would you go and do if you knew that you would absolutely fail, but would do it anyway because the memory of never having tried would cost you your sanity?*

If you allow it, fear will stop you from doing all of the things that you're supposed to do, and from being whom you're supposed to become. And when you decide to let go of your fears and embrace some bold actions in the direction of your dreams, that's when things usually begin to happen for you. It's usually right at the point where you're about to give up, is when everything changes. I challenge you, to be whom you were born to be. To embrace the fear and move forward in spite of it.

Many people don't realize it, but you will remember the best and happiest times of your life as the times where you had to struggle your way through to the finish, but took a chance on yourself anyway. That's when you learn the truth about who you really are. And that is what will make your life story worth telling even more!

Made in the USA
Columbia, SC
17 August 2018